Filming An Indie

A Diary of Making Revenge In Kind

K. C. Bailey

Copyright © 2020 Kathleen Cordelia Bailey

All Rights Reserved

This book contains the personal recollections of the author of events associated with the filming of *Revenge In Kind*.

No part of this book may be reproduced, or stored in a retrieval system, or transmitted in any form or by any means, electronic, mechanical, photocopying, recording, or otherwise, without express written permission of the publisher.

ISBN-13: 9780964493551
ISBN-10: 0964493551

Cover design: The Boland Design Company
Cover Photograph © Pono Productions, LLC

For Angel Vasquez, my Producer and friend.

K. C. Bailey

Table of Contents

CHAPTER 1: DECIDING TO MAKE A MOVIE — 1
- THE SCREENPLAY — 1
- A PERSONAL MORASS — 3
- TAKING THE FIRST STEPS — 6

CHAPTER 2: CONSIDERING MUSIC — 11
- THE POSSIBILITY OF LICENSED MUSIC — 11
- LYRICS FOR A THEME SONG — 12

CHAPTER 3: REALLY GETTING STARTED — 15
- ESTABLISHING PONO PRODUCTIONS, LLC — 15
- LOOKING FOR LOCATIONS — 17
- USING NYX — 20

CHAPTER 4: ANGEL ARRIVES — 22
- MEETING ANGEL — 22
- THE TEXAS FILM COMMISSION — 24
- THE GIFT OF MESQUITE — 27

CHAPTER 5: ANGEL JOINS THE LOCATIONS SEARCH — 30
- THE HOSPITAL — 30
- THE MORGUE — 32
- THINKING ABOUT DEATH — 33
- LEHMAN'S LAIR — 34
- THE GUN SHOP — 35
- A BAR — 36

CHAPTER 6: PRACTICAL CONSIDERATIONS — 38
- SCRIPT CLEARANCE — 38
- THE UNION QUESTION — 41
- CANVASING FOR LOCATIONS — 43

CHAPTER 7: ON MY OWN AGAIN — 45

    LUCK WITH A HOSPITAL — 45
    THE BAR SNAFU — 46

CHAPTER 8: PERSONNEL DECISIONS — 49

    CHANGING DIRECTORS — 49
    CHOOSING A NEW DIRECTOR — 51
    CREW CHOICES — 52

CHAPTER 9: AUDITIONS — 56

    THE ORGANIZING PROCESS — 56
    EARLY SHOO-INS — 57
    LOSING TASHA — 59
    A TURNING POINT — 60

CHAPTER 10: MORE MISHAPS — 63

    CONTRACTS AND A DISPUTE — 63
    LABOR DAY, 2016 — 65

CHAPTER 11: PRE-PRODUCTION BEGINS — 67

    THE TABLE READ — 67
    BUMPS IN THE ROAD — 69
    CHOREOGRAPHY PREPARATION — 72
    CATERING — 73
    SECURITY — 74

CHAPTER 12: THE FIRST WEEK — 76

    DAY 1 — 76
    DAY 2 — 81
    DAY 3 — 86
    DAY 4 — 89
    DAY 5 — 92
    WEEKEND 1 — 96

CHAPTER 13: THE SECOND WEEK — 99

    DAY 6 — 99
    DAY 7 — 103

DAY 8	105
DAY 9	107
DAY 10	109
WEEKEND 2	111

CHAPTER 14: THE THIRD WEEK — 114

DAY 11	114
DAY 12	116
DAY 13	120
DAY 14	123
DAY 15	126
WEEKEND 3	128

CHAPTER 15: THE FOURTH AND LAST WEEK — 131

DAY 16	131
DAY 17	133
DAY 18	135
DAY 19	136
DAY 20	138
DAY 21	139
GETTING AN ALS TEST	142

CHAPTER 16: A FEW MORE DAYS — 144

B ROLL AND THE DRONE	144
ANGEL DOES TIME-LAPSE PHOTOGRAPHY	147
NIGHT DRONE SHOOTING	148

CHAPTER 17: THE OUTSET OF EDITING — 150

ONE DIRECTOR OF POST-PRODUCTION	151
OMITTING THE WORD FUCK	152
THE ACTOR COULDN'T SMOKE	154
BOOM OPERATOR	154
MOVING PROPS	155
FIRST ASSEMBLY	156

CHAPTER 18: MORE EDITING ISSUES — 160

CUTTING THE MURDER OF BROWN	160

CUTTING THE GYM SCENES	162
CINEMATOGRAPHER CRAFTWORK	164
EXTRAS PROBLEMS	165
EDITING OUT ADOLESCENT BEHAVIOR	166
OMITTING THE NAME MESQUITE	167
CHAPTER 19: A POSTER, A TRAILER, AND MUSIC	**169**
HIRING WHEELHOUSE	170
COMPOSERS	172
SOURCE MUSIC	175
CHAPTER 20: SOUND	**178**
HIRING JOHNNY MARSHALL	178
SOUND RUN THROUGH	179
ADDITIONAL DIALOG RECORDING	181
FRIENDLY HELP	183
CHAPTER 21: COLORING	**184**
THE COLORING PROCESS	185
REALLY HARD PROBLEMS	186
THE BEDROOM SCENE	187
A CALIBRATION ISSUE	188
MAKING A BODY DEAD	188
TREATING MYSELF	190
CHAPTER 22: WHAT TO DO WITH THE MOVIE	**192**
FESTIVALS	192
THE DISTRIBUTION RACKET	193
DISTRIBBER	194
OBTAINING SUBTITLES	195
WALLA (AKA MOJO)	196
ALLIED VAUGHN	198
BITMAX, ET AL	199
CHAPTER 23: THE FINAL PRODUCT	**201**
THE DIGITAL CINEMA PACKAGE	202
THE CAST & CREW PREMIERE	202

THE PUBLIC PREMIER	204
REACTIONS TO THE FILM	204

CHAPTER 24: WRAPPING UP — 209

CODA FOR PONO	209
A FEW QUESTIONS ANSWERED	211
WHAT NEXT	214

APPENDIX: LIST OF MY ACTIVITIES — 216

ACKNOWLEDGEMENTS — 221

Preface

This diary recounts the history of making the film *Revenge In Kind*. The feature film, shot in Dallas in the fall of 2016, was released in December 2017. It is a personal memoir of what it was like to make the movie and why I did it.

There are a couple of reasons that motivated me to write this history. One is to fill a gap I saw. When I decided that I wanted to make this film, I looked for books by people who'd produced their own independent movies so that I could learn from their successes and mistakes. I couldn't find what I was looking for, so I vowed that if I finished the film, I would try to write about the experience so that others could benefit from it.

The second motivator is to share the story behind the film with friends and family, the people I love—as well as anyone else who finds it of interest. While it is an exercise in ego, no doubt, it is also a manifestation of giving them some of myself. With that in mind, note that this is a history written from my perspective only. No attempt is made to present others' memories or experiences of the film.

My substory is not integral to the making of the movie, but it is vital to the inspiration for it. Without making it a predominant theme, I will tell of my personal travails that led to the movie's making and which are no doubt responsible for some of the film's and my own mistakes.

Making *Revenge In Kind* was a thrill ride—a roller coaster of hilarious, boisterous highs and nail-biting, cry-in-your-beer lows. Those who want to make a movie themselves may glean ideas from this history; others may find it entertaining. But

K. C. Bailey

before we can dig into the saga of making the movie, it is important to lay out how it all began, which was with a series of personal misfortunes and missteps.

Chapter 1: Deciding to Make a Movie

I grew up loving legitimate theater. I took acting and directing classes, read an enormous number of plays, acted in many, and tried my hand at writing short plays at an early age. Film, however, was not an extension of my abiding passion for theater. So, how I came to write *Revenge In Kind* was not a usual path.

The Screenplay

Revenge In Kind, my first screenplay, was written in 2004. I was in the midst of the best years of my life, living in Hawai'i with my husband, cats, and canary on a small citrus farm. We raised some of our own food and sold a lot to local markets.

Even at the time, I knew my world was idyllic. I kept telling my husband Bob how I adored him and our lives together, and how lucky we were. By day, we'd work on the farm, play golf, and visit the beaches. At night, we'd usually watch the news and a movie, drinking wine and dining superbly on our own gourmet cooking. We talked all the time, he and I, about ourselves, the world, and everything in between. We were lovers, best friends, co-cooks, co-everything.

One of the things we enjoyed was watching all the movies we'd never had the time to see when we were salaried workers. One evening we were watching a film in which a woman was victimized. I found it so upsetting that I had to leave the room until the scene was over. Later on, I complained to Bob that there didn't seem to be any movies in which the woman was the victor, and rapists never seemed to be punished properly. He said that I should write my own screenplay to fix that. Thus was born the idea of *Revenge In Kind*. Basically, it is the tale of a woman who takes it upon herself to punish rapists who have escaped justice.

Because I had no idea how to format a screenplay, my first step was to go online to find books and websites that could teach me the basics. I bought some good software called *Final Draft* and set to work. Having written both fiction and non-fiction books, I knew well how to outline and develop a plot, as well as how to create characters. After a few months of writing and rewriting, I had a first draft. But even without showing it to anyone, I knew it wasn't very good. I thought that the plot held together well, but the characters seemed too pat, too predictable. I put the screenplay aside to think about it for a while. So, it began to gather dust, partly because I didn't know what I would do with it even if I finished it.

Then, in 2005, I saw the movie *Crash*. It transformed the way I thought about film and character portrayal. I'd never seen anything like it. The most appealing element was the multi-dimensionality of each of the key characters, all of whom were individualistic and memorable. *Crash* portrayed how peoples' characters and ethics are often situational, and their actions may not necessarily be predictable based on past behavior. I also very much liked the interchange of scenes and revelation of plot through sequences.

I bought the *Crash* DVD, and over a period of 3 days I watched it six times, writing out a detailed outline of each scene and character. This exercise re-motivated me to finish my screenplay and helped me take a fresh look at each of my characters. Behind every key one, I developed a complete life story—where the person grew up, what the families were like, how each was educated, and so on. My objective was to know each character so well that I could tell you their opinions on anything and probable reactions to any given circumstance. Yet all the while I tried to keep their personal space so that they could act out unpredictably. Then I went back to the dialog and re-crafted each character's style and attitude. At last I had a play and was ready for someone else to read it.

My cousin, Fred Bailey, was a screenwriter in LA, so I asked him if he would take a look at it and he agreed. He gave me some constructive comments to help me tighten the dialog and quicken the pace. In particular, he suggested converting some conversations to action. After another rewrite, I was convinced that I had a really good product.

At the end of that year, I sent out the screenplay to some studios and agents, hoping to strike gold. One hundred percent were returned to sender, unopened. (Later I learned that this was standard procedure because if it had been opened, they might later be sued by some author claiming that the studio had stolen their plot.) This experience reconfirmed what I already knew deep down: to get a foot in the door, you have to know someone inside to open it in the first place.

I thought about making the movie myself but knew that I really didn't have the financial or other resources, especially time. I again put the screenplay back on the shelf where it would remain for another decade.

A Personal Morass

My husband died unexpectedly in early 2012. I entered a period of despair that over ensuing months became ever deeper and darker. It seemed I lived on a different plane from the world around me. Other people carried on with life in a way that seemed surreal to me, while I was keenly aware every waking moment that life would never, ever be the same for me again, for Bob was no longer *there.*

I began to hate. I despised the fat slobs who got to live instead of my Bob, who was fit and trim. I disparaged myself for being the one of us who lived, though I would not have wished the survivor's grief on him.

Also, I began to drink wine heavily and subsisted on dried fruits and nothing healthy. I lost 30 pounds over the next year or so and had no energy or desire to climb out of the hole I was in.

In the spring of 2014, I awoke one morning in the wee hours suffering with what was becoming an increasing problem—horrific cramps in my toes and feet, and nerves jerking in my calves. My toes were splayed, and the outside of each foot turned under, looking like no feet should. The cramps were so hard they made me want to scream, and I worried my bones would break. Grabbing them and twisting hard, I tried to straighten them. It took several minutes for them to relax and I lay back panting. I thought, "This is really, really scary."

K. C. Bailey

What was niggling the back of my mind, and I was trying hard to avoid, was the similarity of these bouts with the onset of my father's fatal illness. He died of Amyotrophic Lateral Sclerosis (ALS), a disease that leaves one's mind fully intact and functional, while causing paralysis by killing motor neurons that enable one to move muscles. It usually strikes people between the ages of 40 and 70 and weakens first the extremities and then finally the chest.

I squeezed my eyes tightly, trying to block my memory of him lying in bed, his mind trapped in his useless body. How claustrophobic he must have been, like being buried alive. And his decline had all begun with the symptoms I now had, feet cramps and leg fasciculations (little muscle spasms). Furthermore, I knew that about 10% of ALS cases are hereditary.

I began to feel ever sorrier for myself. My grief over losing Bob was still an open wound in my soul, yet now there was a new layer to my sorrows. And it wasn't just the belief that I would die soon, a fact of which I admittedly was afraid, but the prospect that it would be from such a terrifying disease.

I thought about going to a doctor to find out if I indeed had ALS, but since I knew that there is no cure for it, what point would there be in being sure I had it? Would I be more depressed knowing I had a fatal disease, or allowing myself the room for doubt? Sometimes not being sure of bad news enables one to pretend things are okay. I decided to give it more time and hope that things would get better.

By the summer 2014, the cramps and fasciculations were almost a daily occurrence, usually in the very early morning. As I became more certain that I had ALS, my depression grew. I didn't want to get out of bed in the morning and was allowing myself to wallow in self-pity. Although I wouldn't allow myself a drink of alcohol before 5:00 PM, I was getting drunk on wine every night.

I was aware that I was in a deep pit, unable to think positively about the future, let alone for the coming day. Even though I thought I had already hit the bottom of my downfall, I was still spiraling downward. But I could not see what to do, let alone how to do it.

Filming An Indie

One morning I awoke with my kitty's head resting on the crook of my arm. She was purring, staring at me. There is something about a cat that always makes me wonder if they are not cognizant of more of the Universe than I, and able to see into me when I myself can't. I lay there thinking about how my life was ebbing away, being eaten by time. I had only an unknown number of days yet to live and I was trashing them with my self-pity and alcohol.

My thoughts turned, as they often did, to the certainty that my husband would be able to handle this so much better than I. I felt his expectations of me in my mind and could almost hear him say, "Kath, don't squander life. Do the right thing." It spurred me to make a decision. I could either succumb to the depression that was consuming me or force myself to get out of bed in the mornings and *do* something. After all, I might not have much time left. I decided to live life as quickly as my stamina would allow and to be as creative as possible.

I thought that the easiest project would use skills I already had—writing and photography. I began feverishly working on a book of my photography and poetry (*Cordelia Bailey Photography* was published in the spring of 2015). I was getting up early in the mornings and working on it almost non-stop during the day. But then, every evening, I stopped promptly at 5:00 PM, when the ogre Grief would again grip me. Stopping work on the book would allow my mind to resume churning with painful memories of loss. I would again dull my existence with wine. Often, I would drink wine instead of dinner, or just have wine and dried fruit and nuts.

After the art book was finished, the single-minded frenzy of creating it was over and I crashed. The leg and feet cramps were no longer just happening at night; they could strike in the middle of the day, making me unable to walk or stand. And I was beginning to feel weak in my hands and was constantly tired. At night, I would awaken gasping for air when I had simply quit breathing.

I decided that that I did want to know for sure that it was ALS. After all, I asked myself, what if it were some other disease that has a treatment or cure? So, I went to the doctor who'd treated my father. His diagnosis: I probably had ALS. Even though I thought I was mentally prepared for this conclusion, I was devastated. I asked him how long I might have to live, and he said that most people live a year or so, like my father had had. Although the diagnosis made me very scared and sad, I knew I now had the choice of living the remainder of my life however I wanted, unlike my Bob who had died so suddenly.

It took a few weeks finally to sort my thoughts, after which I made two decisions. First, I would plan my suicide. There would be no higher priority than making sure I would not be trapped in an immobile body like my father had been. So, I would tell my sister of my problem and secure her promise to help me end my life were I to be unable to do so myself.

Second, I wanted to throw caution to the wind and do whatever I wanted in my remaining time. I thought about how the creativity of writing the book had helped me tremendously. So, I wanted to make a movie from the screenplay I'd written some years before and to be as creative as possible, to have fun, and to not worry about saving for my future anymore.

I concluded that it was okay to spend my life's savings. Since my husband's death, I had been very carefully watching my budget, making sure that I wouldn't be impoverished if I lived to an old age. With my demise looming, caution in that regard became meaningless. Impending death imparts freedom from a host of constraints.

Taking the First Steps

Part of the allure of making a film was to create a product that would outlive me, much like the photography book that I had just completed. But there was one big obstacle: I hadn't the least idea of how to make a movie. So, there was no guarantee that my effort would result in anything lasting. Yet, what difference did that make? Even if I made a mess of it, it would be a blast. It wouldn't matter whether anyone liked it, or it made any money, for I wouldn't be around anymore soon after it was finished. I had the notion that I could make the film in less than a year if I started right away.

I re-read the screenplay that had been sitting around for a decade and saw it needed revision. One issue was updating technology. In the intervening years, communications had changed; people now used cell phones and email, not pay phones. And some jargon was dated. But I was pleased that the basic plot, characters, and dialog were still appealing to me and major revision wasn't required.

Filming An Indie

One of the fun things I did in the update was to change the names of some characters. In the newfound freedom brought about believing I was to die soon was an abandon about offending anyone. I thought about people who had wronged me in life and gave some of their names to the villains. Two former bosses who were particularly unkind to me lent their names to the murderer George Lehman. Likewise, I named people who were heroes after those I liked. I wanted to please my sister Andrea, so I named the lead detective Coxon, which was Andrea's husband's surname.

After the update, which took several weeks working as many hours a day as I could, I sent it to a script-critiquing service and paid for their feedback. Some of their remarks stung, but overall their suggestions were surprisingly good, and it was clear that they'd actually read it and worked to tailor relevant feedback.

After I edited in light of many of their suggestions, I again sent it to my cousin to ask him who could help me estimate the cost of filming it, and for any information he could give me on practical issues of movie-making, like how to go about getting insurance, what I might need an attorney for, templates for contracts, and suchlike. He said he didn't know much at all about managerial practicalities because he had not been involved in such aspects with the films he had worked on. However, he gave me the name of his colleague, Angel Vasquez, whom he said might be able to prepare a "top sheet"—an estimate of how much it would require to make the film as a low-budget movie.

I contacted Angel and he agreed to do the top sheet. I was in a hurry, but I couldn't tell him, "Hey, look, get a move on because I have only a year to live." I had promised myself to tell absolutely no one about my health problems (other than my sister, as noted above) so that there would be no pity or other effects.

Angel promised to finish the top sheet in a month. But after a couple of months, he had done nothing, so I was ready to pull be plug on him in early 2016. Just as I was starting to look for someone else to help me, he finally sent me an answer.

The price tag indeed would take all of my savings, and to stay within that budget, I knew I'd have to micro-manage spending. But that was no problem for me. My entire professional career had involved managing programs, people, and money. Managing things is one of the tasks I do best.

There was a major issue, other than money, that I needed to resolve before moving forward: how much of a role would I play in making the movie, and how much would I delegate to others? Clearly, I didn't have the expertise to man a camera, set lighting, or such practical skills. But I did have a very, very clear image in my mind of how the movie should play. This vision included everything from what the actors should look like and how they should perform their roles, to how scenes should be shot, to what the locations should be like. So, I wanted personnel who would help me make the movie that was already in my head as closely as possible. I was not going to turn over the screenplay totally to the creative capabilities of others, no matter how skilled or successful they might be. For, what would be the point of that if this was to be my swan song, my final thrill ride?

I knew that the easiest way to maintain control of the artistic output would be to direct the movie myself, and I knew I could do it. I had extensive experience in theater and knew a fair amount about directing. Without my even broaching the subject with him, my cousin Fred encouraged me to direct it, which added to my confidence. But there were two insurmountable problems that would cause me to decide against directing it myself. Both related to the filming schedule.

I knew it was imperative to complete production (the actual filming) within 4 weeks, which was not only a normal timeframe, but a budget requirement as well. There would be 12-hour workdays, 5 days a week, for four straight weeks.

The first problem concerned my 16-year-old cat—yes, my cat, whom I dearly loved. Pono was my husband's cat, which made her a link to him for me. She was diabetic. So, exactly every 12 hours, without fail, I pricked the edge of her ear to get a blood sample to check her glucose level, fed her, and gave her insulin based on the reading. There was absolutely no way that I was going to allow the film or anything else in my life to interrupt this schedule, which I considered to be essential to her physical survival and therefore my spiritual stability.

The second problem was my own limitations. I knew that I would be consumed with myriad managerial issues in just making the film and that a hands-on producer would be crazy to think she could also direct. There wouldn't be the time in a day to do both jobs. Also, I was worried I would simply be unable physically to execute the 12-hour-a-day schedule with my health problems.

Having decided not to direct the film myself, I determined to lock the script; no changes in the dialog or plot would be made by anyone without my approval. The final say in any and all artistic output would be mine. Anyone who could not agree to these terms would not work on the movie. I would even put this requirement in the contracts of relevant cast and crew. Thus, I had to find a director who would share my vision and work with me to achieve it.

I first thought of my cousin Fred, who had already helped me with the script, knew it well, and liked it very much. Although he was principally a writer, he had some directing experience so I asked him in April 2016 if he would think about directing the film, but only on the condition of a locked script. He readily agreed.

I asked him for a copy of a director's contract, assuming that he must have had one in the past. I was hoping to use that as a basis for ours so that I would not have to research and then write one myself. He sent me a less-than-one-page contract that was very general. I was surprised at its brevity and called to ask him if he had anything more detailed. Fred said the short form was all he had ever used. I decided to research contracts a little more to see if I could craft something a little less informal.

With the director decision made and feeling confident of myself as producer who could manage the project, I wanted to find a co-producer who knew about filmmaking. An inexperienced filmmaker such as me choosing a producer is akin to a teenager choosing a spouse: you don't know if you will mature in the same direction, or even what to look for to assure compatibility. In fact, the long-term survival of the relationship is less pressing than the need to have it now.

What was I looking for in a producer? It had to be someone who would work for me and with me, and who knew what the job entails. I didn't want someone who needed on-the-job training. I asked Angel, who had told me he'd like to produce on the movie if I were to make it. Not only had Angel read the script and liked it, he had thought about the budget and would have vested interest in seeing it kept in the black. Also, he had a pretty good resume. One of the most impressive things to me about it was not just his past producer experiences, but that he had served in the US Air Force. I have deep respect for military training, and it gave me hope that he could be organized and able to keep schedule and budget.

I asked Angel to come and talk with me face-to-face about working on the film with me as Producer and he agreed. We made plans for him to come to Dallas in mid-April 2016.

Chapter 2: Considering Music

Even as a child I paid close attention to music, especially musicals and movie music. I love how pieces like "Lara's Theme" can convey the romance and spirit of a film like *Dr. Zhivago*, or the soundtrack to *The Shining* can set one on edge with a sort of psychological disorientation. I knew that selecting the music for *Revenge In Kind* would be one of the joys of making the film. The music not only needed to fit the scenes and temperament of the movie, I wanted it to portray the diversity of the characters and the situations in which they became involved.

The Possibility of Licensed Music

Right after I'd made the decision to film *Revenge In Kind*, I began listening to music to select tracks that I liked as examples, and possibly for use. My vague plan was not to hire a composer, which I thought would be too expensive, but to pay to use existing artists and music. First, I would select some, then see what it would cost to use it.

Almost every night, I would sit at my computer, don my headphones and close my eyes, listening to the music as a backdrop to the movie's scenes playing in my head. I was searching for the pulse, the meaningful words, that would give rhythm to each scene—and that would engage the audience on a subliminal level.

I broke my music list into two. The first one was for themes that would go well with key characters. For example, one character, Detective Sam Kang, is from Hawai'i. I wanted to find an upbeat instrumental music featuring the ukulele for him. Another character is a good ole' boy who loves country and western. He needed a solid, simplistic beat that would complement his simmering anger and urge to lose himself in the bar scene.

The second list was for specific scenes. *Revenge In Kind* has a diversity of scenes—edgy and psychotic, playful, violent, and cerebral. For example, an especially important one is a scene in which the psychopathic killer shaves his body prior to a crime in order to leave no forensic evidence. The sound needed to echo his mania and represent the discord of his soullessness and disregard for life. Each scene needed its own accompanying sound to enrich the audience experience.

I spent scores of hours exploring all sorts of recording artists online. I made long lists of singers, bands, and songs. I listened to lots of movie scores, old and new. I searched for a trendy song with the lyrics that would be a good theme. I sorted through voices, looking for just the right timbre and vibe.

I reached two conclusions during these music sessions. One was about a scene in the script, but which was later nixed, in which Coxon and Scott danced. It would show them falling in love, with no words; it would all be conveyed in the way that they danced, the way they looked at and touched one another. The song they would be dancing to, if I could make it happen, would be Bonnie Raitt's *Shake A Little*.

The second conclusion was that I wanted the Italian singer Zuchero to sing the theme song. I researched on the Internet, found his agent and wrote to him, asking if he would ask Zuchero if he would be interested. I never heard back, despite multiple tries.

Lyrics for a Theme Song

In my search for music, I was looking for a song that would capture the mania of the police psychologist as well as the love of her by the lead detective. This was a tough combination. Because I could find nothing that fit the bill, I began to imagine that it would be great fun to have him or her set to music some lyrics I had begun to toy with for a theme song.

Although the main character of *Revenge In Kind* is a woman, I envisioned the theme song as being not from the perspective of that woman, but about that woman. It would be the male lead singing about her and his view of her. Something about her character would be revealed by his portrayal of her and his feelings for her as contained in the lyrics.

Even though I knew her character inside out, and his too, the lyrics were elusive. I jotted them down wherever I was. Once I even pulled over while driving to write down ideas. All the drafts ended up shredded. But I was patient; I knew my muse would visit me. And one day it did, but at an odd time.

I was beginning to have coordination problems physically, sometimes losing strength so suddenly in my legs that I would lose balance. I was scared of falling. My doctor wanted to have an MRI of my brain.

So, on the day of the MRI I was in the waiting room, filled with trepidation about having my body slid into a metal tube. I am enormously claustrophobic, and I was afraid I would panic and ruin the MRI.

To calm myself down, I started thinking about music for the film and I got an idea. I would keep my eyes closed when they slid me in the tube, and I'd keep them closed the entire time to diminish my awareness of being enclosed. To distract myself from my fears, I would write the lyrics for the movie's theme song doing the MRI. Each time I would finish a verse, I would memorize it and mentally recite the whole thing from the top. I would write as many verses as it took to finish the MRI.

It took a lot of concentration, but the ploy worked well. I came out of the tube not only having remained absolutely still throughout the MRI, but with the following lyrics composed and memorized. At the time, I called it *Chris' Song*. The lyrics were later refined, shortened, and adjusted to go with the music. Also, it needed a refrain. But this was the basis.

Babe you took me down
Didn't know anyone could
Now I've got it bad
Didn't know it'd feel so good

Don't know where we're goin'
Guess I don't really care

K. C. Bailey

All that matters to me
Is that I want you there

You seem so remote
Not really here with me
You're on another plane
Like you're floating free

I can feel your heat
And think I have you here
But I look into your eyes
And then I start to fear

You are on a path
I think will sink your soul
Will you take my hand
And let us become whole

I revel in your touch
Your voice, your smile, your mind
I'm taken by your mystery
The answer I can't find.

Fate can mark a life
So time's cleaved into two
Everything's 'fore and after
The day that I met you.

Can you see your way
To give me what I'll give you
My soul, my heart, my me
I just want us to be two.

As for the outcome of the MRI. It showed something called T flares, which my doctor said were consistent with ALS. Ugh.

Chapter 3: Really Getting Started

While it may be boring to some readers, those interested in launching their own film project probably would like to know about some of the building blocks. In that regard, I have included a list of my activities in Appendix A, which could serve as the basis of a checklist for someone doing their own film project. I will discuss a few steps here.

One of the initial objectives was getting legal issues in order. Although I recount the process in a few paragraphs below, these steps are remarkably time-consuming. Not only do you have to figure out what to do, waiting for other people to act can take longer than expected and the process often is slowed by the fact that some things have to be iterative.

Establishing Pono Productions, LLC

I had copyrighted the screenplay in 2005. (You can do this yourself; instructions are online from the US Copyright Office.) But as an added layer of protection of my ownership, I decided to register it with the Writers Guild of America. That was easy, but everything else from this point on required my close attention.

It is important to set up an organization separate from yourself as an individual for protection in event of future lawsuits of any kind. That meant that I needed to create a limited liability corporation for the sole purpose of making *Revenge In Kind*. I decided to name my company Pono Productions, LLC, after my kitty.

Pono means "most excellent, upstanding" in Hawaiian, and was the name chosen for her by my husband. Having a Hawaiian name was emotionally important to me for another reason too. As noted, I wrote the screenplay in Hawai'i, where I'd lived for 13 of the best years of my life. I wanted this film, this project, to have a thread of the spirit of Hawai'i throughout.

On the Internet I found instructions how to set up an LLC in Texas and began filing papers and paying the various fees for registration of the company. Meanwhile, I also obtained a federal employer tax identification number. Once I had the fees paid and the requisite ID number in-hand, I was able to open a corporate bank account for Pono Productions.

The day I walked out of the bank after transferring the first tranche of my savings to the film, I was almost shaking with a mix of fear and relief. Fear, because now I was officially spending my life's savings on the film, and relief that I had finally taken a giant step. Commitment is hard to reverse when one puts up one's money.

From the Internet, I culled a number of models for contracts with crew and cast, and for agreements to use locations, which I used as templates for my own drafts. I was wary, however. What if something were missing from these contracts? It would be wise, I thought, to seek a legal review of my draft contracts.

I called several legal firms in Dallas, Austin, and Houston to inquire about whether they had experience in representing filmmakers or other artists. A couple in Dallas and one in Austin claimed to have such experience.

The first firm I interviewed who billed themselves as "entertainment lawyers" met with me for a half hour in early April. The two of them, a man and a woman, were exceedingly careful to give me no legally helpful information. Maybe they just didn't want to give me anything for free, but the effect was to leave me wondering whether they knew anything about film contracts. The second black mark against them was the price of their retainer, which would be a huge chunk of my film budget.

After I emailed the male lawyer, the junior but friendlier of the two, declining his firm's services, he emailed a reply suggesting that his wife was an independent entertainment attorney who could provide me with two contracts, one for crew and one for cast. I decided to use her services, although they were still expensive at $500.

Unfortunately, the two drafts she provided were boilerplate, poorer quality than what I myself had prepared, had typos, and were almost exactly alike. I was very unhappy, but felt I had no grounds for refusing to pay her fee. What I learned for sure is that attorneys may represent themselves as knowing a subject even though they don't.

I decided to try one more local attorney, who also billed himself as specializing in entertainment law. My previous experience was duplicated, but this time I objected. I called him and said that the two contracts he prepared were almost exactly alike and were the same as what I could pull off of the Internet. He reduced his bill by half, reinforcing what I already knew to be true in life: if you object to people mistreating you, you often get treated better.

After two misfires, I decided that I would forgo an attorney and do it all myself. Later I will explain why this was a mistake and how I narrowly dodged a legal disaster.

Looking For Locations

In addition to setting up the production company and preparing contracts, I began to look for filming locations, which was much more interesting than the other tasks. I began with friends and family, asking who'd be willing to let me use their homes. Almost all of them said yes, but I subsequently found that few of them really meant it. It took me awhile to sort out that they were unwilling because they wouldn't come right out and tell me. They just kept putting off when I could come by to shoot preliminary photographs, or not signing the Location Agreement. (As with the labor contracts, I had prepared the Location Agreement myself, cribbing bits and pieces from several samples I found on the Internet.)

Although a few friends and my sister Laurie and her husband agreed to let filming occur at their homes, there were still not enough locations. There was also the problem that their homes were too nice. We would need some places fitting for a recluse murderer, a student nurse, and a detective. We also needed commercial locations like restaurants, bars, offices, school rooms, and a doctor's office. Let me tell you a bit about the quest for locations for two of them—the murderer's lair and the artist's studio.

In search of a home fitting to a murderer, I finally turned to Airbnb. I thought it would be a snap to find a place, but it wasn't. Often, I would find an Airbnb that was ideal, only to learn that the owner wasn't willing, usually because they'd already had a negative experience with film crews or because they objected to the nature of *Revenge In Kind*. Here is an example.

I found one Airbnb that was fabulous. It was located on the second story of what appeared to be a derelict warehouse. To reach the apartment, one climbed a narrow staircase with steep risers and peeling paint. Inside the very old apartment, the rooms had large dirty windows, ancient plumbing fixtures, and pipes showing. It was just the sort of place you'd expect an evil psychopath to hide out. I knew this was definitely a perfect location for the home of George Lehman, a murdering rapist in *Revenge In Kind*.

As I was talking with the young couple who occupied the flat, they asked me, "Is there anything immoral in the film?" I replied that defining what is immoral is dependent on one's point of view and tried to find out what they meant. It turned out that they didn't want any film that wasn't "Christian in orientation" or that had any "evil" in it. I described the film plot in general terms. They recoiled.

I had to give up that location with a large measure of disappointment. And it always seems incongruous to me in retrospect that this self-righteous couple lived in a place that was such a perfect abode for the evilest of characters.

Finding a place for the murderer would elude me for weeks. Even after Angel came back to Dallas and we searched together, there seemed to be no solution. Eventually Angel would find a place, but even when he did, it would be a bit of an ordeal. I'll say more on this later.

Another interesting experience early on was my search for the art studio of Chris Coxon, the lead detective in *Revenge In Kind*. Although it was clear to me that this character was an artist, I hadn't decided what kind. I really wanted him to be a metal sculptor because I thought it would be a more masculine pursuit, but I knew I had to keep an open mind because the set was more important than the type of art. If I found a really good art studio, it would dictate the type of artist for the character.

Filming An Indie

I enjoyed visiting with many artists around Dallas and seeing their studios. I found it remarkable how many really good artists there are, most of whom are virtually unknown. The investment they have made in their equipment, materials, and space is impressive, as are the storage requirements for unsold artworks.

After seeing more than a dozen studios, I found a man who had a marvelous open-air backyard one under a huge roof. The place was plenty big enough for filming, was well lit, and had a lot of visual interest. The owner was both a metal and wood sculptor. He readily agreed to let me use his studio for *Revenge In Kind* and we struck an agreement for me to pay him a set amount to use his studio for the film, as well as a separate payment for his making a custom, single work of art to be used in the film (to be the artwork of the character).

I handed him the Location Agreement, but he said he would rather have a day to look it over and would call me. He wanted to make sure it contained everything we'd agreed on and nothing we hadn't agreed upon. We shook hands to seal the agreement.

But he didn't call. Finally, I called him to ask if I could come by and pick up the signed agreement. He said he had changed his mind and now wanted 10 times the price we'd shaken hands on. He said a friend had told him it was the going rate for movies to pay for use of a location. When I tried to explain that this movie would not be a big studio production, but an independent with a small budget, he dug in his heels. I decided to move on, that there would be other studios, probably even better ones.

As I mulled what had happened, I recalled something my father had taught me. He said to never to shake hands with someone to close a deal unless I was absolutely sure of it. "Once you shake hands with someone," he said, "it is giving your word. And your word should always be as good as gold." I have always tried to live by that advice, but I realize now that the value placed on a handshake in my father's day is no longer dear.

Fortunately, in May, I found an even better studio with a wonderfully creative potter and sculptor, Rebecca Boatman, who was both genial and a straight shooter. I didn't want to waste weeks again, so I explained up front that we were a low-budget film and that what I offered would be a final sum. I told her she should tell me right then if it wouldn't be acceptable. She was enthusiastic about participating in the art of it all and was willing to sculpt a special piece for the lead character. Also, her studio was beautiful. Her kilns were out-of-doors, where there'd be plenty of room for filming if there were no rain. She signed the Location Agreement.

Using Nyx

Once the deal to use Rebecca's studio was sealed, I needed to address a very important new question. It was now clear that the lead detective, Chris Coxon, was a potter, so what should his artwork would be—the one that he would show to police psychologist Sarah Scott and would ultimately give to her.

The artwork should somehow reflect the character of Scott, with whom Coxon falls in love. Her character has a very dark streak, and she is a very complex and strong-willed person. I decided to use Nyx, the Greek goddess of night. Nyx is one of the most powerful of the pantheon; even Zeus held her in awe.

As I was mentally developing Coxon's motivations for choosing Nyx as the model for his sculpture, I wrote a poem that I imagined he composed to Nyx. I even thought about adding it to the film somehow, but it didn't really fit. Nevertheless, I share it with you here. Everything it says about Nyx is drawn from Greek mythology.

Nyx, Daughter of Chaos,
Goddess of the Night.
Your children give us Grief,
Death, Deceit, and Strife.

You bring upon us Sleep,
And our crimes you can conceal;
Yet it's only due to you
Stars of Heaven are revealed.

Filming An Indie

Your power is so great
Even Zeus is sore afraid.
You're the only goddess
Whose word he must obey.

After I had talked with Rebecca about the statue, she also researched Nyx and came up with a fabulous design for the bust, one that clearly brings to mind Nyx for anyone who knows of her. Rebecca then made two copies in case one were to break accidentally during filming. It turned out to be a great experience to have Rebecca's creative input and talent on the project. And her enthusiasm was very energizing.

I had hoped to film Coxon actually firing the sculpture of Nyx, but I wasn't too keen of his just placing her in a commercial kiln. I remembered that when first visiting Rebecca's studio that I had asked her about a big trash can with holes in it. She had explained that she sometimes used it to fire pieces, although the "trash-can kiln" wouldn't reach the required temperature to sufficiently alter the clay to make it lastingly hard. That was okay with me; I liked the idea of using visible flame. I had it in mind to use the firing scene as the opener to the movie.

Ultimately, I decided that opening the film with the firing of Nyx was too much of a visual non-sequitur to follow with the violence that needed to occur early. So instead I placed it elsewhere in the movie, but also used it as the background of the languages-selection menu before the movie begins.

Before moving on from Nyx, let me recount a side-story. Rebecca first promised to have the Nyx sculpture ready on September 2, 2016, which would leave breathing space before filming was to begin September 18. In August, however, I learned that Rebecca was going to Burning Man and would not be back until September 11, when she would then finish Nyx. I had two thoughts. First was, "Oh, dear, would there really be time to complete Nyx after she returned?" to which I told myself not to worry, we could always set aside the Nyx idea and use a substitute statue. The second was, "Burning Man, how wonderfully appropriate to the spirit of the movie and the scene."

K. C. Bailey

Chapter 4: Angel Arrives

I had already started working on the film but was doing so without the expertise I needed. Angel, who would produce the movie with me, was coming to hopefully provide what was needed to professionalize the process and to make sure we really could make a film that would reach completion. Angel first came to Dallas in late April 2016.

Meeting Angel

As I drove to the airport to pick Angel up, I thought about how I didn't even know who he really was. I had not seen his photo; I didn't know his race, physique, or personality. Here I was, having a man come and stay with me about whom I had so many questions. What if he were a thief? A slob? A psychotic? A cat-hater? Too obese to sleep on my guest air mattress? In fact, all I knew about him was that he liked my screenplay, had a relevant resume, and was once a work colleague of my cousin's. But my cousin had told me nothing about Angel as a person and I'd neglected to ask. Adding to the uncertainty, I had no idea of how long he was to stay, whether it would be a couple of days or more than a week.

I felt a little crazy, second-guessing myself as I drove to the airport. Then I felt a moment of giddiness. This is what this movie experience is all about, I told myself—doing something whacky, unusual, and daring. I was throwing caution to the wind. I was no longer the conservative 66-year-old widow; I was a filmmaker! I would greet this unknown person and try him on for size. Would he help or hurt my cause?

Filming An Indie

Angel knew what type and color of car to look for, so he flagged me down. When he got in, my first question was whether I should use the English or Spanish pronunciation of his name. He said Spanish (which I later learned no one else would use, so I don't know why he said that). Then awkward silence ensued, punctuated only by mindless chit-chat.

Angel did not put me at ease, nor did I him. Practical matters crept into my thoughts, displacing the heady notions of the half hour before. Was I going to have to feed this guy every meal, treat him like a guest to be served? Would I have to pick up after him all the time? I had no intention of waiting on anybody. And what about money? Would he pay his way? Would he do his own laundry?

My apartment had two bedrooms, the smaller one of which I used as an office. I was used to getting up at 4:00 AM, taking care of Pono's insulin and food, then working on my computer for several hours. With Angel sleeping in my office on an air mattress, things changed. The hallway bathroom became his, and one half of my dining table became his office. The tiny kitchen was shared, as was the shower in my master bathroom.

For several years, I had lived alone and suddenly I was sharing half of my personal space with a male roommate whom I'd never met. But our relationship got off to a fairly smooth start because he was extremely tidy, considerate, and sensitive to my preferences. He also shared in the cooking and cleaning. I couldn't have asked for a better-mannered guest. But still, as it turned out, we were both very private people set in our ways and preferences. There were many small steps to work out before we could dance together.

We started building our "film relationship" right away. Although I told him nothing of my illness or my time limit of one year, he understood my goal of making the experience a like a thrill ride; that I wanted to make it memorable and fully participate at every level. He also understood my knowledge limitations and set about helping me formulate steppingstones for the pre-production and production phases of the filming.

One of the first questions Angel asked was what I wanted to do with the film once it was finished. I wasn't going to tell him that I wouldn't be around then, so I just told him the first answer that came to me: I wanted to show it in film festivals. The fact, however, was that I didn't care very much what would happen after I finished it. My focus was the process, not the ultimate disposition of the film. But, of course, he was right to be asking the question.

We spent every day together for almost six weeks—far longer than the week or so that I'd imagined he'd stay. And it was odd because we never even discussed when he would go. We just got up and worked on the film every day.

One morning as I prepared to leave my bedroom and go into the dining room, where I knew I'd find Angel working on his computer, I thought to myself, "This is akin to language immersion. We two have been thrown together in close quarters and are learning one another's personality every waking hour."

I learned that we had some things in common. We both love good food, but have a special weakness for quality pizza, and quality booze. We both exercise, although he more than I. And we have tremendous respect for animals. Even our political views and senses of humor are not far apart.

But communication, unless it was over food, was sometimes difficult. In particular, he didn't like to be interrupted when he was on his computer and under his headphones. The problem was that I was working away in my office and frequently needed his advice or approval on things. So, there was some friction as he expressed his annoyance and I would feel a bit resentful.

The Texas Film Commission

Despite the delay on the contract and a few other things, we did move out smartly on other topics. One was a priority relating to the overall budget, the possibility of getting help from the Texas Film Commission (TFC).

The TFC had a program that offers about 10% back of money spent in Texas for films that employed Texas residents as 70% of their cast and crew. This would have a huge beneficial impact on the budget of *Revenge In Kind*, so I wanted to make sure that we qualified and applied for it. I was emphatic about this with Angel when he first came to Dallas and we even put it in his contract.

Filming An Indie

So, one of the first things Angel did was to make an appointment for us with the head of the Dallas office of the TFC. In preparation for the meeting, I sent a copy of the screenplay to the director of the office, along with a list of what we would like in the way of specific help.

We wanted not only to qualify for and obtain the incentive, but also wanted help with film locations, a point of contact with local police (to help answer questions related to authenticity), and contacts to get necessary permits. We knew that there were others who had filmed in Dallas and wanted to make use of what we assumed were well-known procedures and contacts.

We arrived at the TFC on the morning of our appointment and were greeted by two very somber, almost glum, young men who showed us to a conference room. They sat with us and made polite but minimal conversation. They wouldn't answer many questions, telling us to await their boss, who was running late.

When the office director, Janis Burklund, finally bustled in and sat at the head of the table, she was scowling, clearly a bad sign. We made introductions, then she got right to business. She said she had read the screenplay while she was on an airplane back to Dallas the day before. The look on her face was as if she'd just eaten something that tasted rotten. I was somewhat taken aback that she actually made a face, which I thought was unprofessional and judgmental.

She proceeded to tell us that the plot and some of the action in the film were repugnant and that she didn't think that the film would be something that "the City of Dallas would want to be associated with." She was particularly put off by the fact that a rapist has his penis cut off in the film.

I was shocked. Could it really be that the TFC was exercising censorship, trying to determine what the content should be of films made in Dallas? Would she really deny us help with the film because she objected to the screenplay? As it turned out, the answer to both was yes.

Before the meeting ended, we asked for help in interfacing with the Dallas Police Department (DPD). She said, "I can assure you that the DPD would turn down your request, based on the nature of your screenplay." She proceeded to dampen our expectations of any help whatsoever, and especially the prospect of any financial help, regardless of whether we could meet the requirements of the TFC Incentive Program.

Indeed, her predictions were accurate. And I feel that she guaranteed the outcome herself. Early the next morning, we received word from the TFC that the DPD had declined our request to film outside their headquarters, to provide a point of contact for advice, or to help us in any way whatsoever. I found this to be remarkable not only with regard to the speed of the reply, but to its comprehensiveness. I couldn't quite believe it.

I decided to call the DPD Office of Public Affairs myself. I explained to the DPD representative on the phone what we were doing, the nature of the film, and asked if I might have an appointment with her to discuss DPD help. She was very friendly and agreed readily to see me. We set an appointment. However, before that meeting could ever take place, it was inexplicably cancelled, and my calls were no longer returned. I surmise, of course, that the nice woman learned of the opposition to our project by the TFC.

Angel and I thought that we might be able to end-run the Dallas office of the TFC if he went to Austin to see the head-office TFC office personnel. So, he took the bus down there and made our case for funds from the Incentive Program for the film if we met all of the requirements. He came back to Dallas hopeful.

Soon afterward, we were told by the Austin office that there would be absolutely no funds available to us from the Incentive Program. In fact, we were told that we needn't even file the paperwork because, although the fiscal year in which we'd film was still 6 months away from starting, all monies had already been committed to other projects.

Although the TFC would provide us with a little bit of non-financial help over the course of the project—such as to post our job openings on the TFC website—Angel and I agreed early on that we could not depend upon the TFC for important help. After receiving misleading information from the TFC in a couple of instances and lack of response in others, we both became somewhat paranoid about TFC. We also decided that we wouldn't respond to any requests from TFC about our film or our progress. We were afraid that TFC would sabotage our relationships with people and organizations we'd need around the city.

Interestingly, the TFC continued to seek information about where we were filming, what resources we were using, and what film permits we sought. Because we knew that they'd be of no help in any respect, we didn't respond to emailed or phoned questions from TFC staff on such issues. When TFC wasn't able to get information from us directly, Ms. Burklund called one of our production assistants to try to get inside information about our filming activities and the locations we were using. Upon learning this, I ordered everyone on the film to give TFC no information whatsoever and to direct any incoming call from TFC to Angel or me. I could think of no good reason why Ms. Burklund would want to know our filming locations.

The Gift of Mesquite

After the negative response from TFC, we were fearful that we would not be able to film very easily in Dallas. Angel suggested we think about nearby towns within the metroplex. One of the first alternatives that came to my mind was Mesquite, to the southeast of Dallas.

The City of Mesquite turned out to be pivotal in making the film. Not only did it allow us to use many locations on City property, their officials facilitated the filming in a host of ways. Having Mesquite's help was magical. It all began with James Mack.

James Mack, then-Manager of the City of Mesquite Arts Center, was someone with whom I was acquainted because I had worked with him with on a few art exhibits at the Arts Center in the past, and I had an upcoming show of my photography there scheduled for the fall of 2016. After realizing that we wouldn't be allowed to use locations owned by the City of Dallas, I emailed Jim to ask if we might speak with him regarding the potential of using the Arts Center as a base for the film. He agreed to talk with us.

Jim was very practical, businesslike, and a strong supporter of all the arts. When Angel and I met with him, he expressed willingness to let us use a large room at the Center for our base of operations for 6 weeks. He also said we might use sites within the Center for filming. But both came with one condition: we first had to obtain a filming permit from the City of Mesquite. This was absolutely the break we needed.

Getting a film permit from the City of Mesquite was difficult and time-consuming. It required filling out a detailed form with three fields of information. One was to provide a precise list of planned film sites and times. This scared me. What if it rained on the day we wanted to use a bus stop, or an actor was sick on the day we were supposed to use him on a specified location? Would Mesquite let us change the schedule around? The detailed instructions of the form led me to believe that they expected us to know what we were doing and when, and stick to it. But I didn't want to ask, which might be interpreted as our being unsure of ourselves.

The second field was for references. These were easy to provide. The hard part was reaching all of the people to let them know that Mesquite would be calling and why. Too many were on vacation or otherwise unreachable. We wanted to do this before we turned in the form, so this chewed up about a month.

The third field was for stringent insurance requirements. I needed to nail down our insurance a little quicker than I'd anticipated, which meant I needed to fast-track my learning curve. I will come back to the insurance issue later, as it was a pretty important component of the preproduction action. For now, suffice it to say that many days were required to research and select the insurance we needed, and to make sure that it complied with the prerequisites of Mesquite. This took a lot more work than I had planned for. Getting the Mesquite paperwork all filled out properly took about 6 weeks and continued between Angel and me well after he had left Dallas that first trip.

Then there was the waiting on pins and needles for the answer. I really felt that I might have to abandon the film project if Mesquite said no. It was that crucial. We had tried and failed to find a back-up alternative in the intervening weeks.

Once Mesquite agreed to give us a filming permit, it was like casting off the dock and unfurling sails. The joy I felt when that permit was finally in hand was over the moon. We had a headquarters as well as a location for filming more than half of the scenes. Not only were we being allowed to use the Arts Center in Mesquite, but also the City Building (a gorgeous structure with great production value) both inside and out, and city streets. My gratitude to the City of Mesquite knows no bounds. Without their support, *Revenge In Kind* would not be the quality it is and probably would not even have been made.

Chapter 5: Angel Joins the Locations Search

While Angel was still in Dallas during his first trip to see me in April, we focused on trying to find film locations for five key scenes—a hospital, morgue, house for our murderer, gun store, and bar. I had already found places to film regular "house scenes" and had put together a list for outdoor shots, so these five were the ones that would be most difficult to nail down.

The Hospital

Finding a hospital room was crucial. There is a scene in the movie where the murderer goes after being shot and the police interview him. It is really the only scene in which this character has much dialog and it is very revealing of his personality.

While you can fake a hospital room with a bed in a stark setting, to me it always looks unreal. I can tell instantly in any film whether the room is not in an actual hospital, or else there wasn't a budget to build a credible alternative. Maybe I have visited too many people in the hospital, but there are things that I expect to see like oxygen spigots on the wall, vital signs monitors, red electrical sockets indicating generator power, and just the look—almost the medicinal aroma—of a true hospital room in the US.

Before we had fully realized that the TFC would be of no help—and might even be harmful—we asked them if any other movie made in Dallas had successfully obtained agreement to use a hospital room for filming. We hoped that such a location, having had experience with a film crew, would be open to our using them too. We were surprised and pleased when the TFC said they'd look into it for us.

Filming An Indie

This interaction occurred fairly early in the process, when Angel was in Austin trying to rekindle our prospects for participating in the Incentive Program. While there, he received word from the TFC that they'd arranged for us to meet with Parkland Hospital personnel. I was very hopeful about this because Parkland had just relocated to a new building, leaving the old one boarded up and unused. The empty old building, scheduled for demolition, would be a perfect location for us.

To arrive on time to the appointment the TFC had set up for us at Parkland, Angel had to catch a 4:00 AM bus out of Austin to hurry back to Dallas. He arrived tired but eager. We went straight to Parkland from the bus terminal and asked for the man we were supposed to meet.

When we began to talk with the man, it became apparent that he was a volunteer whose job it was to orient visitors to the public spaces of the hospital. He said he knew nothing about filming and hadn't been told of our objectives. We knew there'd been a major misunderstanding somewhere and we hoped it was at Parkland and not at TFC.

We got the man to take us to his boss, who told that us that the TFC had mentioned nothing of our desire to use the hospital for a set and that they'd only been asked to give us the usual "public orientation" of the hospital foyer and shops. He told us that there was no precedent for using Parkland as a film location and that there was no way we'd be able to use either the new or the old hospital for a location. We cut short the "meeting."

Angel was as angry as I ever saw him get. When he asked the TFC why they'd arranged an orientation session instead of facilitating our using the hospital as a film location, the answer he got was that the TFC is not in the business of helping us locate film sites. "That is the job of a locations scout," the TFC Dallas Director, Ms. Burklund, emailed us.

That was snide, given that we'd already told her that due to funds limitations, we were doing the locations scouting ourselves. And it was futile to point out the email exchanges with her that fully documented our only reason for going to Parkland Hospital — to obtain a shooting location. The TFC knew that they were wasting our time with the Parkland "orientation" appointment. It was just plain mean-spirited. This is when we vowed to not ask the TFC for further help.

The Morgue

In addition to a hospital location, Angel and I were searching for a credible venue for a scene that is supposed to take place in a pathology lab where autopsies are conducted. In my imagination, it was starkly lit, had several stainless-steel tables, refrigerator drawers for bodies, and equipment that was genuine. I spent hours phoning the Dallas city morgue, funeral homes, and hospitals. But my calls were fruitless; nobody wanted a film crew at their facility. So, we started looking at places that were not actually morgues, but which might be suitable with tweaking.

One of the facilities we went to was rather strange. It was a company that prepares dead bodies for shipment, mostly overseas. The director of the facility explained to us that most of their "clients" are visitors to Texas who die while here and have to be returned to their home countries.

He showed us a room with a couple of sloped tables with buckets below and hoses running from the low part of the tables to the buckets. Bodies would be put there and drained of their fluids and then double-bagged, hermetically sealed, and placed in containers for shipping.

The place was poorly lit, with scarred and dirty concrete flooring, and the equipment was not at all right for what we needed. Angel proposed that we pay to paint the floors, rent the right equipment, and do our best to make it work. I decided not to spend the money and time.

Before Angel had even left town, we had both run out of ideas on what to do about the morgue. One evening soon after our visit to the cadaver packager, I made a decision. Sometimes you have to give up your preconceived notions and revamp the scene if you don't have the right location, especially if it is not one integral to the plot. The pathology lab was such an example. Although it would have added great production value to have a real pathology lab, the amount of time being devoted to the search was out of kilter with the short length and importance of the scene. I decided to rewrite the scene to be one which takes place in a hallway outside of the lab.

Thinking About Death

Night was not a rational time for me, particularly after the ALS diagnosis and especially since I drank too much wine every evening. The night after searching for the morgue was particularly bleak. I lay in bed in the dark thinking about the slab in the body shipment facility. I pictured my own dead body there, devoid of motion or color.

All of the millions of humans on earth will face death, and many of them, like me, will have foreknowledge of how soon it is likely to occur. How many, I wondered, lay in the dark like I did, feeling the fear of the unknown? It is so lonely. Have they all felt loneliness like mine? You can say the words, "I am afraid. I don't want to go away and be nothing. I want to see what happens in the world." But it doesn't capture the trembling turmoil you feel. There are no words for the terror of peering into the abyss of being forever gone.

Maybe others are not so afraid because of their beliefs. I have known for most of my life that religion is very useful in facing death. Being able to believe in an afterlife assuages the fear of nothingness with the salve of promise—promise of not having to really end.

I lay there thinking that living life is absurd really. You spend years gaining knowledge, nurturing love, and (for many anyway) becoming tolerant and forgiving. Like annealed metal, the internal stresses dissipate, and strength grows with the fires of experience. Like aged wine, taste and balance improve with passage of time. Then you die. So, what's the point of all that experience and wisdom?

Then the lyrics came to me, "What's it all about Alfie? Is it just for the moment we live?" Yes, that's it, I thought. It is all just for the moment we live.

Inevitably, these morose mental meanderings ended up with me being full of self-pity. I wanted my husband back. I wanted to lay my head on his shoulder and tell him of my fears. He would stroke my cheek, hold my hand, and tell me that what really matters is that we have this moment together and that we really and deeply love one another. Thinking about him is when the tears would drip. With his death, there was no solace for me and no one for whom I was number one.

Like the non-sequiturs of a dream, my thoughts would zig-zag back to pondering the Big Picture. All of the religions with large followings have some sort of explanation of the meaning of life and most deal with the notion of hereafter. They ascribe options for continuance, despite the fact that without brains there won't be thought; without bodies there won't be eyes to recognize or hands to touch. And, in my experience, there'd never been evidence to support any of the assumptions or tenets—claims of heaven, nirvana, reincarnation—of these religions.

I was willing to admit readily my own limitations of imagination. The biggest example of my inability to conceptualize was my lack of understanding of what is beyond the Universe. A box has a wall and interior, and there is always an exterior. So, the universe should seemingly have an end, with something beyond it. Okay, so the Universe is expanding, and I somewhat can grasp that concept, but what is it expanding into? What is beyond space? Since I couldn't answer this, I had to be an agnostic rather than an atheist.

Most nights, my thoughts would gradually move from hurtling here and there to a calm. On this particular night, I was lying on my right side as the peace of near sleep came over me. I laid my right hand, palm up, on the bed and pretended that Bob was there and that he reached out and put his right hand on mine as he used to do. I was struggling to picture it visually and to "feel" him. Soundlessly, my cat Pono curled up next to me and put her paw on the palm of my hand. It was electric. Evidence? Hmmm.

Lehman's Lair

Angel and I had spent a lot of time talking about the house for our murderer, which Angel dubbed "Lehman's lair." We felt it had to be small, but with enough room for the film crew, and should be spartan. I told him about an Airbnb I had seen online, and we set off to meet with the woman who owned it. Both of us really liked it and it fit our criteria, but when we told her that we wanted the place as a film set, her price immediately quadrupled. No matter how we tried to get her to budge, she felt she knew "the going rate for film companies".

We wouldn't locate the murderer's lair until much later, but there was one good thing that came out of the visit to that Airbnb. In a corner of the bedroom there had been two marionettes. Instantly I knew that they would fit well with the murderer, whose name was George Lehman. Marionettes were how Lehman saw people—disjointed, malleable, breakable, inanimate.

I asked the woman if she would rent the two marionettes to me. She declined. After we left, I told Angel we absolutely had to find some for Lehman. He said, "No problem, just tell the production designer."

The Gun Shop

Finding a gun store proved difficult also. There are not that many gun stores in Dallas that are film worthy. We needed a shop that had enough space to allow for good camera work and that had an expansive supply of firearms to make the scene authentic.

Before Angel arrived, I had visited them all, including some pawn shops that had large firearms collections, and found 3 that would work and whose owners were open to the idea. (Initially I found 4, but someone drove a huge truck into the gated plate glass front of one right after I had visited it and stole all the firearms inside, putting it out of consideration.)

When Angel came, we went together to pick one of them. Angel thought one was too small and located too far away, so it was out. He liked the second one best and it was okay with me. It was not only large enough to handle the film crew but had a nice vibe to it. We made multiple visits and worked for a few days on getting the location, which entailed lengthy conversations with one manager, and then another.

Unfortunately, there were two insurmountable problems: it would require our renting generators because of their electrical limitations, and they wanted several thousand dollars for just part of a day. They had been used as a location for *Walker Texas Ranger* and had been paid $5000 for that, so they expected us to do the same. We had to take a pass.

The third gun shop was my favorite. Upon entry, one walked through several rows with shelves of ammunition to reach the counter that had gun racks in back of it. The walls were covered with gun ads and signs. We wouldn't even have to decorate the set.

The first day I'd visited the shop, the owner had not been present. However, when I took Angel to see it, the owner was sitting outside in a rickety chair with a couple of local men. When we walked up and Angel told him that we were scouting for a film location, the owner was delighted and turned to his companions to tell them, "This is the one! This is the movie that will film in my shop!"

It turned out that his shop had been considered by a couple of films, including *Walker Texas Ranger*, but had never been selected, to his regret. As we left the shop that day, Angel told me that there was no way we could back out of using this shop, given how happy we'd made the owner by selecting his place for the film.

I was really glad it worked out too because there were resident cats who lounged on the counters. Being a lover of all felines, I thought it lent character to the shop. I would have been happy for them to be in the film, but on the day of shooting they of course made themselves scarce.

A Bar

During that April visit, when Angel and I searched so diligently for locations, we visited dozens of bars looking for the best one for a scene in which a rapist is shooting pool and bragging about his conquests to a disbelieving patron. The place had to be a dive, a honky-tonk sort of space with either a single pool table, or one that was fairly isolated from others.

The bar turned out to be the one location about which Angel and I had the biggest disconnect in our visions of what we needed. Angel was quite taken by a big cavernous bar on a highway well outside of town. He liked it because it was a downtrodden place of the sort the movie's character would visit. It had lots of neon lighted signs on the walls, pool tables, and a huge U-shaped bar.

I didn't like it. I was worried about the place because of acoustics issues and the fact that it was open 7 days a week, morning to night, so we'd have to contend with patrons' noise and potential interruptions. Also, I didn't like the fact that it was miles away from town and transportation would be time-consuming. Although Angel was insistent that we try to book it, I dragged my feet. My preference was for a cozy bar, but also with enough room to enable good camera work.

In all, during Angel's first visit, we drove more than 1000 miles around Dallas searching for locations. (That was in addition to the 700 miles I had driven finding the locations we already had and preparing the list for when Angel came.) I was glad that we started early because it took 5 months to finish finding all but one of the sites. And the final site, which Angel eventually found, was a cliff-hanger—more about that later.

Chapter 6: Practical Considerations

Angel and I would spend our evenings talking over what we had accomplished and what remained on our list. He was a fount of information. He was never quite sure what I knew or didn't know, so he asked me a lot of questions.

Script Clearance

One evening during that April visit, he asked me whether I had arranged for script clearance. "Say what?" I responded.

He explained that I had to have someone qualified read the script to identify all possible legal conflicts associated with, for example, business or product names. This script clearance enables one to obtain Errors & Omissions (E&O) insurance, which covers liability and defense for the film company against lawsuits alleging unauthorized use of titles, ideas, plots, plagiarism, invasion of privacy, and several other perils. Most film distributors will want to know that the script has been cleared and has E&O.

Realizing this was pretty important, I began searching for a specialist who knew how to do script clearance and, most importantly, could produce the requisite certification letter for the insurance company. This turned out to be a harder process than I'd imagined.

An Internet search revealed a few firms advertising that they conduct script clearance. But they had very little information, such as cost or what their certification letter included, online. They didn't just answer phone calls; I had to make appointments with each for telephone conference calls. It took several days to finally interview 3 of the firms.

All wanted between $1100 to $1600 for the job, but there was a huge stumbling block: none would give a clearance letter "that could be used as a legal document" of the sort that insurance companies required for E&O. I couldn't understand why someone would pay so much money for a clearance that couldn't be used legally.

I decided that maybe I was being too restrictive on getting a "legal document," so I called the insurance company I was thinking of using, United Agencies. Sure enough, a *legal* letter would be required for the E&O insurance, which itself would cost $5000 for just 3 years. So now I was looking at an unexpected expense for the E&O, as well as the problem of finding and paying for the legal letter. This was not only frustrating because of the time being chewed up, but also it was adding to the growing budgetary concerns.

I heard that there was a professor who taught entertainment law at Southern Methodist University who did script clearances, so I emailed her. She telephoned me and said that, although she could not do it, she advised me strongly to get a lawyer not only to do the clearance, but to help with all my legal affairs. She reinforced something I had already learned: attorneys will portray themselves as "entertainment attorneys" although they have little or no experience in the business. She also warned that contract templates on the Internet can omit some very critical language, so I should beware.

Her advice rekindled doubts I had about the contracts I'd crafted using templates on the Internet and whether they contained all the necessary clauses. So, I asked for her recommendation of an attorney and she gave me the name of a large entertainment law firm in Los Angeles. She said, "It won't be cheap, but this is one expense that you need to find a way to afford." I knew I would follow this advice because it reminded me of something my father once told me: "Movers and shakers will at some time or another get into legal fights. I want you to remember this—never, ever allow yourself to be out-lawyered." (I was forever pleased that my dad thought I might someday be a mover or a shaker.)

Before we rang off, she gave another piece of advice: hire any important crew members yourself, as you will need both their loyalty and a personal link with them. My not adhering to this last principle would return to haunt me. (More about that later.)

The needs for a legal letter on script clearance and help on making my contracts correct were again forefront in my mind. My hesitation about paying for an LA firm was exacerbated by the fact that no money had been put in the budget for either legal fees or insurance, and I had been too inexperienced to notice. The insurance, aside from E&O, would total about $10,000, even with a high deductible. Here I was worrying about whether we could meet budget and we were less than a month into the one-year project.

There was an inexpensive insurance alternative, Angel said. An acquaintance of his worked for an insurance company and he would agree to put us as a "sub" on another insurance contract for another film. That acquaintance would then issue us "certificates of insurance" whenever we needed to prove we were insured.

I asked Angel why anyone would be willing to do this and whether we would actually be insured, or we would be just paying for the certificates. Without really answering the question, Angel assured me that the practice is common and the only route available that was affordable.

This solution sounded risky, so I decided to ask the United Agencies representative about such a scheme. The United rep told me that people may do that, but it is not legal because the "top layer" firm that really is the insured party doesn't know about it. Also, if you ever need to file a claim, you can't. There was no way I was going to pay for such fake insurance.

Next I called the recommended large law firm in LA. After consulting with them about what they would do for me, I assented to their (for me) huge retainer and sent them the script for clearance. And, because I had decided to do things the "right" way, I bought the insurance from United Agencies and set in motion the process for getting E&O as well.

The script clearance, when it was completed, was interesting in one regard: I had to change the name of a character. My new lawyer had done a search of the movie's characters' names in a couple of data bases and had found that one was the same name of a man still doing time in prison in Texas. Since his crime was similar to the one committed by the character in *Revenge In Kind*, there was a tiny possibility that someday he might claim that the movie was about him and that he was thereby defamed.

The Union Question

Another early question Angel asked me was whether the film would be a union production. I really hadn't thought about it and answered, "Well, I certainly want to treat people according to union guidelines and payment. I won't overwork anyone or mistreat them."

He explained that mistreatment wasn't the question. The essential question was whether I was going to pay the union its own take in order to assure that the film wouldn't be "flipped."

Flipping is the practice whereby an independent film might be started in a right-to-work state, but then cast and/or crew threatens to walk off the job right in the middle of filming unless the production is immediately unionized. In such a situation, the producers would then be faced with two options. One is that they could cease film production. Alternatively, they could accept delays while things are worked out, face the psychological effects of the flipping on the cast and crew versus management, and absorb the financial implications.

I asked Angel how much it would cost to make the production unionized. He didn't know, so we decided to go and talk to the local office of the Screen Actors Guild – American Federation of Television and Radio Artists (SAG-AFTRA).

When we met with SAG-AFTRA, I was totally straightforward. I said what I wanted to do, how much money I had to spend, and asked what the additional costs would be if I were to make the production unionized.

The answer was startling. The costs would be roughly 25-30% more if I were to make the production union. And, I would have to put the funds for salary payments into escrow before the start of production. I said I needed time to think things over and went home to do calculations.

After doing some math, I called my cousin Jeanette, who is a set decorator for major studios and a firm believer in unions. I told her that I thought I could barely make the film with the funds I had but didn't want to get in the middle of production and then be shut down by the union.

"Do you have any ideas as to what else I could do here?" I asked.

She encouraged me to pare back expenditures on the film somehow and to go union. She said, "They already have you in their sights now that you have visited them and told them your plans. You probably will be flipped."

Several weeks passed during which I did my budget calculations over and over. Angel had left Dallas and I knew I had to make a decision. After doing the budget math one more time, I concluded that the two choices were to either make the film without the union, or to abandon the project. So, I decided to go see SAG-AFTRA one more time to see if there were any other in-between option I hadn't considered.

Meeting again with the union rep, alone, I laid it all out again, but this time in more detail. I explained that I was fulfilling a dream and that the money to do the film was all mine, and all I had. There were no other deep pockets I could turn to and no one else was helping me. I said I would treat everyone as fairly as I could and that at least the cast and crew would get to have the experience of a feature film, perhaps even one that could be successful enough to help their careers. I said that the financial cost of making the film unionized was prohibitive.

The union rep was true to her responsibility. She tried to talk me into going union and paring down the film budget to accommodate. She would make no promises regarding whether my production would be flipped and left me with the feeling that this would happen should I proceed without going union. I went home feeling very apprehensive.

I emailed Angel with the information I now had about the full budget implications. He considered everything carefully and concurred that there was absolutely no way we could go union and still make the film. He left the decision to me, knowing it was my money we'd be gambling with. I said I was prepared for the loss.

We decided to make sure that everyone knew that the production was non-union, non-guild before they were hired. And I put a clause in all contracts stating this clearly. We also made it clear that we would follow union rules as closely as possible. Not only was it the right thing to do, it was perhaps a way to forestall disgruntlement. That decision made, I also mentally prepared myself to abandon the project midway in event they decided to flip us.

Whether it is true or not, I shall forever believe that SAG-AFTRA considered flipping my film but decided not to, for which I am indebted and grateful. The film would not have been possible otherwise, and I thank them for letting my dream become reality.

Canvasing For Locations

One night over dinner, Angel and I discussed the fact that we were not getting the locations lined up as quickly or well as we had planned. Angel suggested that we put together a flyer and go from house to house in not-so-good neighborhoods offering to rent a house for a few days.

The next morning Angel gave me a draft flyer and I worked on editing and printing it. By late morning, we set out to a neighborhood not far from the Mesquite Arts Center. Houses there were quite small and most of the structures looked like they were built in the 1940s.

It was sweltering as we went from house to house, leaving the flyers. At one place, a man was tearing up floorboards in an empty two-bedroom place that he was renovating.

Angel saw gold. He talked to the guy, who immediately agreed to rent it to us for a week in September, but warned us, "Some of the floor won't be replaced yet, but there will be joists." Angel said no problem, we would put down plywood.

The plan was for me to return the next day with a Location Agreement for him to sign. But when I did, he wasn't there. I tried calling the number he'd given us, but it was disconnected. One more dry hole.

A day later we drove down a street nearby the dry hole and saw an old pickup backed to the front door of a house with a yard of sunbaked dirt and thigh-high scraggly weeds.

Angel said, "Let's see what's going on here. Maybe this is it." As we opened the car door the smell hit us even before we could identify the whine of a thousand black flies swarming over the bed of the pickup.

"Hello?" I called. An old, stooped black man came out carrying a load of trash and dumped it in the pickup, causing the pitch of the whine of flies to rise.

We talked to him a bit, learning that he had been hired to clean out the place after a renter had fled without paying rent or the electric bill. The electric company had shut off the electricity and, because the refrigerator was full of food, everything inside had rotted. He said he thought there was also a dead animal inside, but it was so decomposed he wasn't sure what it was.

Angel asked if I wanted to look inside to see if it might be a prospect. I wanted to say no, but then thought to myself, "This is part of it all. And what if this is the place we've been looking for? I have got to do this."
I did it. I felt like I would retch from the smell.

The effort turned out to be in vain. Later, when we phoned the number the old man gave us for the owner, he said he wouldn't rent it to a film crew.

Chapter 7: On My Own Again

Angel left Dallas in May to tend to his personal business and prepare for returning in a couple of months to stay until the production would begin. I began a period of working alone, particularly on continuing the search for locations.

Luck With A Hospital

I decided to make one last full-scale effort to get a hospital room. If I were not successful, I would need to rewrite that portion of the script and find another way to reveal the content of that scene. I half-heartedly revisited a few hospitals, both large and small, then started checking nursing homes, going to more than a dozen. For varying reasons, no one wanted a film made at their facility.

One day while in Mesquite, I went to the Dallas Regional Medical Center (DRMC), which had previously been a scratch. Luck was with me and I got to speak with the Director of Emergency, Lisa Fox, who surprised me with being open-minded to the idea of using the facility for the film. She asked for a presentation, one describing the film and exactly what we wanted to do at the facility, that she could submit to her administration to seek approval.

I raced home and devoted a couple of days to composing a PowerPoint with supporting documentation. In record time, I emailed it to Fox and also delivered a hard copy to her office. Then began the wait. I had to restrain myself because I wanted to call her every day to ask if we had permission yet, or any news at all. Yet I did not want to be a pest.

Meanwhile, I kept looking for alternatives, but other options either were not amenable or fell through for other reasons. In the end, the DRMC was my only hope. I was on edge for 4 months until we finally got a Location Agreement signed with DMRC in early August.

When we ultimately filmed the hospital scenes at DMRC, we got to do it in an empty wing, where we wouldn't disturb the mission of the facility. Lisa Fox, and her colleague Darlene Morton, also participated as extras in the scenes, doing a superb job playing the professionals they are. (Aside: I was very unhappy that the camera work filming the scene with Darlene did not show her. Not only did she deserve to be shown, it would have been more realistic to have her in the scene.)

The Bar Snafu

Angel and I had not agreed on the type of bar we needed and we both rejected the other's findings. So, I tried to think of what would be an in between bar and reinitiated the search after his April visit.

I was looking for an "upscale dive bar" and thought I found the ideal one in the Lakewood section of Dallas. This bar had more of the atmosphere I thought Angel wanted, but also fit my own requirements regarding size, an isolated pool table area, and a long bar.

This bar also was a good possibility for us because the guy behind the bar at noon, when the place opened, said he was the owner of the business. We had had so many problems trying to find the right person to talk to at any bar we had considered that I almost interpreted this as a good omen. (Or, I would have if I believed in omens.) Anyway, I felt that if he were to agree, there would be no additional hurdles in getting a legal Location Agreement signed.

The owner was eager to have the film at his bar. He even asked if he could be in the film as an extra and agreed readily to the sum I was offering. He signed the Location Agreement on the spot. The interaction was so smooth that it was almost too good to be true, which bothered me.

Also, something about the man made me uneasy. He had hard, unfeeling eyes. There was a snide undertone to his conversation that portrayed his sour view of life and mankind. I had a sense that he would double-cross his mother and anyone else when it suited him. I decided that I would look for a backup bar in case he changed his mind, although I had no inkling of why he would.

The next bar I found was equally good, Belzie's Bar. It had an isolated pool table and sufficient room. And, like the Lakewood place, the business owner was there. He also agreed to the sum I offered and said he would sign the agreement after his attorney looked at it. I left him with a copy, asking that he call after he'd had it reviewed.

I returned to Belzie's a few times over the next three months trying to get a signed agreement but was unable to close the deal. He was always either out or was well into his day's drink. Lakewood looked like it would be the film site, without a backup.

I am going to jump ahead in time now to let you know how close we came to a disaster with the Lakewood bar and why a backup turned out to be a film-saver. During pre-production, less than a week before we were to begin filming—with the very first scene scheduled to be filmed at the bar—I took some crew to Lakewood to do measurements. I had tried unsuccessfully to reach the owner to tell him we were coming by but thought it should be no problem to visit during the bar's open hours.

When we entered, the crew began looking for electric sockets near the pool table. The woman behind the bar asked what the hell was going on. I was outside and was called in to talk with her.

It is hard to describe the level of animosity she projected when I told her that the owner had agreed to let us film at the bar. She said, "No way. I am co-owner of this joint and I agreed to absolutely nothing."

No amount of kind words would warm her up or calm her down. She didn't say the deal was off, but I was pretty sure that she would try to end it. I felt a slow burn of panic arising in me.

I tried to call the man who'd signed the agreement but couldn't get through to him. I had a really bad feeling that the Lakewood bar would cancel, so I scrambled to reconnect with my alternative on the back burner, Belzie's Bar.

Fortunately, I reached Belzie's owner's assistant, who said that, yes, the film could still be done at the bar starting on the next Sunday morning. I went by to get the Location Agreement signed and made arrangements for the bar to be opened for us at 5:00 AM, with a promise that we would have it to ourselves until 2:00 PM, the normal opening time on Sundays.

I felt it was quite a coup after the prolonged struggle of getting Belzie's lined up. But there was an unsettling problem with Belzie's too: they wouldn't agree to a backup plan in case the person to open up on Sunday didn't show. I knew 5:00 AM was awfully early for these people. I begged to have a key or a telephone number of someone to wake to no avail.

My fears about Lakewood had been justified. Saturday evening, 12 hours before we were to begin filming, the guy from Lakewood finally contacted me. He emailed one sentence saying that I was no longer welcome to film at his bar.

That I'd judged his character correctly was little consolation. My guess is that he'd never told his partner about the film and had planned to pocket the location fee we were paying. At any rate, I was relieved that I had gotten Belzie's as a backup.

Chapter 8: Personnel Decisions

Choosing the people who work on a film is one of the most important decisions made in the entire process. If you get people who are not talented and trained in their craft, they taint your work. If you get cantankerous people, they can derail the esprit de corps. As a life-long manager of programs and people, I knew this well. I tried especially hard to get the best I could for the limited money I had.

Changing Directors

As noted earlier, I chose my cousin Fred to be director of the movie. He was my first hire after Angel, and we signed our contract in early May 2016.

Fred was very familiar with the script, having commented on a couple of earlier drafts, and was very enthusiastic and supportive of making it a film. I thought that having someone I'd known all my life and trusted, who had some directing experience, and who loved the script "as-is" was perfect luck.

A few weeks after we finalized our directing contract, I got a surprise call from Fred. He informed me that he'd re-read the script and had extensive changes he wanted made. And they were very, very substantive, involving not only revision of dialog, but plot and character as well. He even wanted to write in a role for his young boy, for which there could be no reasonable plot justification. I was extremely taken aback because he had previously praised the script as being in great shape and had consented to its being locked.

I badly wanted to keep Fred as director because I was comfortable with him and trusted his experience. To lose him would be a setback to the film as well as to my psychology at this point. I asked him to send me his ideas and I would see if I could accept going in the direction he wanted to take the film.

With his notes, I went through the script yet again, making any of his changes I felt would not impact negatively on the film. I was determined to try to meet him halfway, but in the end, there were too few of his suggestions that I could accept. In my opinion, he wanted to convert a highly realistic drama that examines life issues into a more lightweight action story.

One of the more objectionable changes Fred wanted to make was to open the film with a shot of a raging bull running loose down a street in Dallas. I asked him, "Setting aside the cost and difficulty of making such a scene happen, what is the relevance to the plot? And it is so unrealistic that such an even would happen in Dallas, what is the point?" He had no answer that I could fathom. Additionally, and very importantly, some of his changes seemed to undermine the power of the strong female lead, which was an essential element of the story.

After I re-edited script, accepting as many of Fred's changes as possible, I sent it back to him on June 5 with a "Screenplay Agreement" for him to sign. It said that said he understood that the script was locked, just as a play for stage often is, and that he would be willing to proceed with it as-is.

I kept wondering to myself what the reason could be for his U-turn. Had he just decided that he really didn't want to direct it, so wanted to terminate by making unacceptable demands?

My next call from him was anticipated but nonetheless made me very sad. He said his suggested changes were imperative, was adamant that the script was horribly deficient, and said it had taken him until now to realize it. He said some deflating things, including that I would be wasting money to make a film out of the script as it stood. If I were unwilling to accept his changes, he was no longer interested in directing it. And so, we parted ways.

This event was seminal. I realized that I was so confident in the screenplay that I was willing to part with Fred rather than change it. And subsequent to our phone conversation, I was able to slough off his harsh criticism. I realized I truly and deeply believed in the merits of the script.

Fred's newfound negativity about the script also had some impact on Angel. They spoke by phone after Fred quit. Afterward, Angel said we needed to better define "the character arc" of the players and wanted to invite others to critique the script. He was voicing the exact same complaints, and even using the same vocabulary to describe them, as my cousin had. I replied that if there were a problem with the script that ever became evident, certainly we would all support fixing it. But for now, we needed to forge ahead based on what we had. In coming weeks, as more participants who joined the project praised the script as exciting and well-crafted, Angel's concerns dissipated.

There was a silver lining to losing Fred because no one else on the film would be as important to me as he was. The event inured me to even the thought of losing any other staff on the film at any later point.

Choosing A New Director

Angel was a big help to me in coping with my loss of Fred. His attitude was that "these things happen on a film" and you have to just keep moving onward. He immediately set out to find another director. He had several resumes and talked to me about some of the prospects. One that interested both of us was Roger Lindley.

Roger lived in Amarillo and had some directing experience. We decided to have him read the script and then have a telephone conference call in mid-June. Roger was very impressed with the script and enthusiastic about making the film, but when I told him that the script was locked, he said that wasn't acceptable. He wanted to be able to change the script if he thought it necessary, so he declined the directorship. Angel and I went back to the prospects list.

Unexpectedly, Roger called me the next day with a proposal. He would make revisions he'd like to make to the script. I would review them to see what I could accept, then we'd talk. Neither of us would be under any obligation. It was a no-lose proposition. I thought that was fair.

Roger's suggestions were not radical, thus were mostly acceptable to me. He suggested no revisions to the characters or basic plot. And I had a good feeling about him as a person; I simply liked him. It was wonderful to have found such a promising director within only a few weeks of losing Fred.

We three decided to hold auditions starting in mid-July. In the interim, Roger and I traded a number of thoughts on the script as we tweaked and reached a closer understanding with one another on the project.

One of the issues I was most keen on was to make sure that Roger viewed the character Sarah Scott as a complex, simmering, and slightly crazy woman—but one who is totally competent and driven. So early on, I emailed Roger a few thoughts that I had written down during the period in which I was developing Sarah's character. He seemed glad to have them and was interested in trying to reveal the edginess to her personality coupled with the strong personal and psychological dimensions. Through such interactions, I was really feeling good about Roger and felt that we were forming a team.

Crew Choices

I had wanted to get started on selecting crew in early May, but Angel first wanted to have his LA attorney review the contract between the two of us. That review took a very long time and I became quite agitated at the delay. When Angel finally signed the contract, it was late June, at which point we had to enter into a hurry-up mode on getting crew. We were about two months away from the start of pre-production (the week when staff would assemble to prepare for actual shooting).

The late start was a negative in two related ways. First, it limited our pool of talent to people who had not yet committed themselves to other jobs during our production period (scheduled for September 18 – October 13). Second, it forced us to make decisions quickly without sufficient time for checking references or considering how people would work together. Looking back, I would never do this again. I would rather let production slip than be forced into a hurry-up mode when selecting crew.

Filming An Indie

On June 30 we really got moving. Angel had identified all of the crew positions that were absolutely required, eliminating any jobs we could do ourselves or have others do. Then he posted a crew call online.

To receive the crew call responses, I set up an email account on the Pono Productions Google Drive. I then made folders for each job title and filtered every applicant daily. As emails came in, I placed them into a job folder along with a ranking of their qualifications for Angel's review. It required reading, categorizing, and responding to hundreds of emails, a process that took me several hours a day for over a month.

One of the first positions filled was to bring on Zubi Mohammed as Production Manager. He was Angel's friend and would become his right-hand man. He worked closely with Angel to decide whom to interview for the crew and how much to offer for each position. Once someone accepted our job offer, Angel gave me their information and I drew up a contract.

On positions like gaffer or grip, I was not qualified to weigh in, so didn't. Other jobs—like production designer, cinematographer, production manager—were very important to me, so I took an active role.

The production designer is the one who determines how sets are laid out and dressed with props and lighting, including the color scheme for the costumes and sets. Since I already had the movie playing in my head, I wanted someone who would not only help bring that vision to reality, but who would add their own layer of creativity and spice to the vision.

The position of production designer was the first on which Angel and I had disagreement. The first woman we interviewed in person had two marks against her. She spoke very softly with a thick accent. I am extremely hard of hearing, and her speech was nearly unintelligible to me. The second problem was that we'd given her the script to read in advance, but she said she hadn't had time to look at it before our first meeting, although she'd had it for over a week. Angel felt she was highly qualified and within our price range, but I said we needed to keep looking. It was a good experience for me because it helped narrow what we were searching for.

One of the next people we interviewed, this time by phone, was D.R. Garrett. She almost blew the interview because she talked nonstop, making questions hard to get in. But listening to what she said, admittedly in way too many words, pleased me. She'd read the script, had definite opinions about what she'd like to do, yet was very open to guidance and collaboration. I also liked that she understood budgeting and how to keep track of expenses; she struck me as being both an artist and a capable manager. She proved to be both.

Filling the cinematographer position was more problematic. Angel began the process by asking me to identify films that I liked. He used that information to identify possible cinematographers in our price range, then asked me to watch clips from their reels. Angel is an amazing walking dictionary of films; he has not only seen hundreds, he remembers them and details about their production. This knowledge came in very handy when we were trying to narrow down what I liked.

Angel found two cinematographers whose work really impressed me. One was in Texas and the other in Alabama. The Alabama guy, my first choice, kept not returning phone calls and emails, thus he disqualified himself over time. The Texas man was willing and able and both Angel and I wanted to offer him the job, but first wanted to check it with Roger, whom we'd just hired.

Roger balked, saying he wouldn't work with the man. I asked Roger if he'd ever met him and he said no, but that he knew of his reputation. He wouldn't even interview the man experimentally, which bothered me. Nevertheless, I bowed to Roger on this because it was imperative that he work well with the cinematographer. We considered a few others, but they were not ideal by any metric.

Soon it was the second week of August and we had only 2 more weeks before pre-production was to begin. I was worried about a bundle of issues, but at the forefront was choosing the cinematographer. Angel then suggested a woman with whom he'd worked in the past, but whose experience was very limited. Her work samples were suitable, and she was available, but my interview of her was lackluster. I felt very unsure, but Roger and Angel convinced me to hire her. Angel assured me that she had all the necessary basic skills. Beyond that, what ultimately mattered to me was that Roger was comfortable with her and she was responsive to him.

Looking back, it is pretty amazing that we put together a team that worked well and was exceedingly professional in such a short time. We had only two months to select the crew and I think we were remarkably lucky to find such outstanding people.

Chapter 9: Auditions

In early July, Angel asked me to put together a list of the types of actors we needed for all of the roles, specifying desired age range, gender, race(s), and physique. I realized that the movie that had been playing in my head was populated almost exclusively by white people. I felt embarrassed, so I set about identifying which roles could be open to any race. Angel then posted the casting call online on July 7. We went live! I was so very excited when the applications started coming in.

The Organizing Process

Much like with the crew call, I set up Google Drive folders into which I sorted the reviewed resumes and headshots as they came in. We received scores of resumes, fully half of which were from people with no or inadequate qualifications. I put together a form letter to send to these applicants that offered an opportunity to be an extra in the film.

For the applicants who had potential, I requested video samples and put these into the Google Drive folder as well. Then Roger and I ranked them. When we both chose someone, that person was automatically invited to audition. For others, Roger and I went back and forth a bit, leaning toward including people in the auditions if either of us had strong preference.

We decided to try to fit all of the auditions into one week in late July. Angel is an absolute ace when it comes to doing things on the computer or Internet, so he set up a sign-up sheet online for the people we'd chosen. We had a lot of people coming in scheduled back-to-back, morning to evening. For those out of town or unable to come on the days we were auditioning, we set up a process either to audition them via Skype, or to receive video readings.

A couple of days before we were to start auditions, Angel asked me who was going to be the reader for the actors—the one who'd say the lines in the script not being spoken by the person auditioning. Well, I hadn't thought of that. Furthermore, there was no money itemized in the budget for such assistants.

I looked through the applicants to find some young people who wanted to participate, but who had limited or no credentials. I found 5 who were excited to help with low pay. They were the readers as well as assistants with the auditions. I was happy that later one actually had a role in the film, another became a set decoration assistant, and another served as an extra. Their willingness to take on a limited, small job led to greater participation and thus some experience in film.

Another thing that I was glad I did was to make a rating sheet to record our evaluations of the actors. I'd learned to make such sheets many years before in one of my managerial jobs. With auditioning so many people each day, it would be difficult to keep them sorted in our minds. Even more important than these rating sheets, however, was that Roger videoed each audition. We ended up relying very heavily on reviews of those, especially later when our first-choice actors were unavailable, and we had to go to back-up candidates.

Early Shoo-Ins

I was not expecting the wide range of capabilities the candidates displayed. Some were awful, but some were so superb that selection was open-and-shut.

One of the first videoed auditions to come in was from Tasha Dixon in Los Angeles. She read the classroom scene in which the police psychologist recognizes that a student is emotionally struggling with the lecture topic of rape. Dixon's delivery was spot-on, and she had a quirkiness to her expressions that held a hint of the craziness that underlies that character. Also, she had a strong physique, so I thought she'd do the action scenes very credibly. I told Angel I wanted to hire her for the lead actress, and we began discussions with her.

Meanwhile, Roger happened to be in LA and met with her. He was a very strong supporter of choosing her as well. I thought that the decision had been made and accepted and moved on to other roles. That wasn't accurate, but more on that later.

Other roles were not so open-and-shut. Two of the ones about which I was most worried were the leading man and the lead bad guy. For the former, I hoped for someone not overly young, who fit my definition of handsome, and who could masterfully portray the range of emotions that his character would need to express. For the bad guy, we needed a tough guy who could project craziness coupled with craftiness, and who could come across as psychotic, but brilliant.

We were well into the auditions, and I knew we had a problem. Not only had we not found anyone for those roles, there had not been anyone who would even do in a pinch. I resolved that I was going to have to think about somehow coming up with money to fly in actors from LA and put them up at significant expense.

Then in walked Chad Halbrook—handsome and young, but not too young. Physically he was definitely what I had in mind. "Please let this guy be good," I silently begged. As Roger proceeded to put him through his paces, it was hard to keep from grinning. Not only was he good, he was exceptional. I thought, "This guy can carry the movie if he has to." Roger and I didn't even have to confer; we both wanted him.

The second role that I thought would be hard to cast was the really bad guy. I knew he had to credibly convey being evil without reliance on dialog. He had to look and act insane, even when he wasn't harming anyone. In particular, there is a scene where the character gets off on watching a video of violence. If an actor could pull off this one, I would know we had our guy. I asked Roger to have those who auditioned for the role do this scene, which entailed no dialog, just pure acting.

There was a fellow from Austin, Tom Heard, who'd had a hard time reserving an audition spot online. He called me, irate about it. He was ready to give up, but I tried to be even keeled and help him get in. I was ever so glad we persisted in setting him up for audition.

When Tom entered the room, I noted he had the physique I was envisioning, but did he have the talent? I sat quietly and watched Roger work with him, but I didn't think

Roger was testing him very hard. At the end of the audition, when Roger hadn't yet asked him to do the "getting off" scene, I spoke up and asked for him to do it.

When Tom Heard finished that part of the audition, I couldn't restrain myself. I jumped up from behind my table at the back of the room and rushed up to hug him. "Fantastic!" I exclaimed. He was sweaty and still breathing hard from the exertion of the scene, but I had to hug him one more time. Roger said, "Hmm, I never saw anyone hug an actor for his performance before." But I thought that Roger agreed with my sentiment.

Perhaps the oddest audition we had—and there were a few—was a guy who came in to try out for the lead detective. Roger would ask him to play a scene in a hostile way, then with a mild manner, then with another emotion, and another. In almost every case, he just delivered the lines in a monotone with almost no variation in response to Roger's requests. But in one instance, the guy erupted and said the lines with a venom (and flying spittle) that the content could never justify.

I kept waiting for Roger to cut it short, thank the guy, and say the usual, "We will be in touch." But he didn't. He decided to have the guy stand up and go to the corner, then enter the stage and say his lines while entering the scene. The guy staggered while walking and slightly slurred.

After he had finally left, Roger said that the guy was possibly a very, very brilliant actor. "No matter what his instructions, he kept playing it the way he saw it," Roger said. I replied that the guy was on drugs and that there was no way I would want him on the set, let alone in the movie.

Losing Tasha

Near the end of the audition week, we had almost all of the roles cast. Then we hit a bump in the road. Tasha Dixon, whom we'd settled on for the leading woman, said that she'd need to come back to LA midway through production, so we would need to arrange the filming schedule around her schedule. I was unwilling to do this not only because there were locations that might not be available if we planned around her needs, but I also worried that if she were introducing this change now, after we'd pretty much nailed down the contract, she might make other changes later. If so, that could be a death knell for the film. With great sorrow, I decided to cut her loose. So, we began the search for a leading lady once again.

We went through all the "almost good enough" resumes again, but they still didn't make the grade. We cast a wider net locally, and also asked our Production Director, Zubi, to help us find someone. Zubi is remarkably well connected. I think he probably knows more people in film than I have known, regardless of profession, in my whole life.

One afternoon Roger and I were auditioning an actress via Skype. Her resume had looked really good as had her photograph. But what she hadn't said on her resume is that she has a thick German accent. I tried to cut off the audition right away on that basis, but she protested that she could do almost any accent, even Russian (although I couldn't understand the relevance of mentioning Russian). To give her a final chance, I said, "Okay, play the scene again using a Russian accent." She said she couldn't just now because she'd have to prepare. "How about American English?" Same answer.

I mention this one example just to show how exasperating two phenomena in casting are. First, people don't always reveal key things about themselves in their resumes that would save everyone a lot of time (because they wouldn't get the audition, which is of course why they don't reveal it). Second, they outright lie about their capabilities. You have to put them to the test right away to filter them out.

After rejecting literally dozens of applicants, in came a video from an actress whom Zubi had found, Sasha Higgins. She played the role very well and was beautiful to boot. I loved that she didn't have dyed blond hair like half of the actresses, and she had very expressive eyes. I said, "Roger, how about Sasha?" He agreed. We were a little worried that she didn't have the weight and physique for the action scenes, but she was very committed to training intensely for the fights. It was a relief to have Sasha on-board.

A Turning Point

Roger, Angel, and I were working very well together during the auditions. I felt true synergy. But on the last day of auditions, there was an event that was to be a major turning point between Roger and me that would affect the remainder of making the film—in fact, it would affect our entire future relationship.

I arrived in the auditions room, which had been moved to a smaller upstairs location for the final days. Roger and Angel were there, conferring quietly. Roger stood and asked if he could talk to me alone. Then he looked at Angel and said, "KC and I have something to talk about." Angel nodded, as if he already knew.

Roger and I went to a nearby conference room and sat. He said, "There can be only one director on the film." I replied that I was well aware that there could only be one director but opined that we had worked well as a team thus far and could continue to do so. I reiterated what we'd talked about at the outset, that I had a vision for the film and that he'd agreed to help me achieve it. He kept repeating that I needed to let him do the directing alone.

I was thinking fast. I knew I wanted to be able to tell him my ideas, which he might or might not accept. At the same time, I wanted him to "own" the directing. He needed to have artistic freedom to put his own layer of creativity onto the film. I decided to let the reins loose and ride wherever the horse took me, so to speak. I said, "Roger, I get it. I need to stand back and let you do the directing. I promise I will." He seemed satisfied.

I really didn't know where this conversation originated, but I could only guess that either my having asked Tom to do the "violent video" audition had bothered him, or that Angel had told him he needed to have this talk. I vowed to myself to take a very, very hands-off attitude during the filming. I definitely wanted him to be invested in the film and to not get in the way of his freedom.

One of the first times Roger's admonition affected my actions was with our lead actress, Sasha Higgins. Sasha had arrived from LA during pre-production to work with our stunt coordinator and choreographer. Sasha was very gung-ho about the role she was playing and asked me if we could meet so she could understand her role from the writer's point of view. I agreed, but immediately felt apprehensive. What if she asked me questions relating to how the role should be played, which was a question for the director, not me?

Sasha asked many good questions about my intent for the screenplay and clearly had thought about her role a great deal. She had a few questions about how I envisioned the role being played. I demurred, saying that Roger would be talking to her about it.

In retrospect, I wish I had been forthcoming with Sasha. What I would have said is that the character has an imbalance which enables her to take on the vigilante role. Sasha portrayed this attribute in some scenes, particularly toward the end of the movie, but I think if we had talked about it, she would have had it as a stronger thread to the way that the character is played throughout. So, the mistake I made is not giving open, honest answers from the perspective of the screenwriter.

Roger's conversation with me had a huge impact on our relationship as well as my own behavior and decision-making. There would be many times when I had suggestions that I would like him to consider, but I would remain silent. But overall, I knew he was absolutely right; there could be only one director of production, just as there could and would be only one director of post-production.

Chapter 10: More Mishaps

In August, I realized that we had postponed way too many jobs and decisions. We were getting overwhelmed. The days were not long enough and our energies not sufficient. Also, some poor decision-making on my part, as well as unforeseen events, came to haunt.

Contracts And A Dispute

It was August and I had created dozens of now-signed contracts with crew and cast. I had been so very busy with long workdays that I'd had no time to worry again about whether I had got them right. Then I had a conversation with my attorney in LA, the one who was doing the script clearance. She suggested that she review at least one of the contracts to make sure it was complete. I quickly sent her an example, regretting that I'd waited so long. I worried that she would find an error and cringed at the thought of having to re-do all those contracts.

My attorney called me a few days later with some bad news. She said that I had neglected to include some key elements, one of which was absolutely crucial—a remedies clause. A remedies clause says that even if a cast or crew member seeks legal remedy to a problem, they can't enjoin or restrain the exhibition, advertisement, distribution, or other use of the motion picture as relief. In other words, someone could sue me, but they couldn't kill the project in the process. This clause, she said, was so important that no distribution company would touch the film without it.

The wind went out of my sails. I knew I now had to re-do all the contracts. Not only did I have to spend hours redoing them, I had to take the time to explain to each person the reason they needed to sign all over again.

Now let's jump ahead 10 months in time so I can tell you why I was so glad that I got the legal advice and acted on it. The movie had been through post-production and had premiered to cast and crew in early June 2017. I was now fully engaged in doing preparations for marketing, including a poster, for which I had hired a professional trailer house, Wheelhouse Creative in New York. (More about this later.) I then posted the draft poster on the private *Revenge In Kind* Facebook page I shared with interested cast and crew for their comment.

From left field came a totally unexpected problem. Shortly after posting the draft poster on Facebook, I got a call from one of the lesser-role actors who informed me that I had promised him that his name would be on any movie poster for the film and demanded that I follow through. I told him that I had no recollection of such a promise and that I didn't think it would be appropriate for such, given the level of his role. He persisted, saying that I would soon hear from his lawyer.

Indeed, shortly thereafter I got an email from his lawyer threatening that if I did not put the actor's name on all posters, he would seek to enjoin any distribution of the movie. He cited the first contract signed by that actor, which didn't have the remedies clause. The actor hadn't told his attorney that he had subsequently signed a revised contract *with* the remedies clause.

Rather than interact with the actor's attorney myself, I asked my attorney to address the problem and sent her a copy of both of the contracts signed by the actor. She called the actor's attorney and shared with him the contract that contained the remedies clause. The actor's attorney readily agreed that this foreclosed the actor's option of closing down distribution.

I shudder to think what would have happened had I not followed legal advice about the contracts. I would have been blackmailed into placing a lesser actor's name on the poster just to assure film distribution. And who knows what else he might have demanded in return for not shutting the film down?

Filming An Indie

Labor Day, 2016

Roger and I had plans to meet at 8:00 AM in my apartment to spend Labor Day going over the script in fine detail. We were going to make sure that we had the same vision of the scenes and get each other's ideas on how they were to be filmed. Unfortunately, this plan was derailed by events.

Just after midnight, I awoke with cramps in my feet and difficulty breathing. After drinking some water, massaging my toes, and propping myself up against the headboard, I tried to fall back to sleep. Had the pains not awakened me already, I would never have seen my phone light up. (I am deaf without my hearing aids, so couldn't hear my phone.)

I put on my hearing aids and answered the call. It was an automated voice telling me my dear niece, whom I love very much, was incarcerated. The recording instructed that I should call a number (at an exorbitant fee) using my credit card. I did so and got through to her.

She had been arrested for drunk driving and was still so under the influence that she had no idea which jail she was in, how or when I could bail her out, or what time her arraignment would be. She pleaded with me to come and get her.

I told her she would have to wait until morning, but that I would come for her as soon as was possible. Then I lay awake for hours, fretting about her and angry that the time for review of the script with Roger would be lost. My great comfort was that she was not hurt and had not hurt anyone else.

A while later, I got another call from my niece saying that I would need to bring $1000 in cash for bail and that her arraignment would be some time in the morning. I got up early and went to find an ATM, but it would allow me only $500 per 24-hour period. I then took my checkbook to the only place I could find open, a grocery store, and asked them to cash a check, but they wouldn't.

When it was time to meet Roger, I told him of my problem and asked if there was any way he could loan me $500. Graciously, he agreed, and we found another ATM. He then accompanied me to the jail where I waited to pay bail.

K. C. Bailey

Although we tried to work on the film some, I was not able to do it well. I had been awake seemingly for days and certainly all night. The impact on the film is, of course, unknowable. But for sure it obviated an opportunity for Roger and me to build a closer working relationship, and we lost an opportunity to gain mutual understanding of the purpose and nature of key scenes.

Chapter 11: Pre-Production Begins

The week before filming actually began, key people arrive to prepare. This is the time when the cinematographer meets with the crew to go over the locations, the production designer begins work with the property master to prepare for the sets, logistics are planned, and the shooting schedule is finalized. It is an enormously hectic period that enthralled me completely. I felt like I was in a whirlwind with the level of energy around me so alive that it was electric.

The Table Read

Although September 12 was the first day of the one-week pre-production period—the week of preparation before filming begins—it really all began on the 10th with the table read, which is when the cast got together around a big table and read their roles straight through the script. The purpose was not only to enable the cast to meet and get a more realistic feel for the script, but also to help me spot any problems with it before we started filming.

We met in the Black Box Theater at the Arts Center, which was a large room with tiered seats rising from the floor-level stage on two sides. The black walls made the space cozy, but the high ceilings kept it airy. There were only about 40 cast and crew members who could make the event, so there were many empty seats. Even though it wasn't crowded, it was my first moment of seeing a large group of people gathered for the single purpose: make *Revenge In Kind* into a film. I was thrilled to have made it this far and was interested in seeing the faces of the people who would put the next creative layer on the project.

Before the table read began, I stood on the stage to offer a few welcoming remarks. Although I am very used to public speaking and have no stage fright, my pulse was up. I could feel the eagerness coursing through me. Here it was at last, the opening moments of actual movie making.

As I looked at the faces of cast and crew, I thought how blank they looked. Did they feel excited too? I began with telling them that this is the culmination of a long history for this screenplay. It was now moving from words on paper into their hands. Now they would apply their layer of talent and artistry, turning it into a work by many rather than a dream of one.

After welcoming, I turned to a practical matter: I talked about something that Angel and I were worried about—keeping the cast and crew healthy. Both of us feared that influenza or even a bad cold could bring down the production, so I urged that anyone who became ill should, for the sake of the movie, let us know so that we could limit the exposure. Although most of their faces revealed nothing, a few looked at me askance, as if I must be kidding.

Roger then took the floor to welcome everyone. At the end of his remarks, he said that "None of us are getting paid what we are worth…" at which point a woman (whom I later learned was a strong union advocate) loudly said, "That's for sure!" Roger went on to say that all of us should give our best despite the low level of pay. I felt it unnecessarily set a bad tone, so later I asked him why he made such a remark, to which he replied that he was only telling the truth.

Our table for the read was set in an open-ended rectangular U around which the actors sat, with the leading roles set in the center. There wasn't enough room for everyone, so the smaller-role actors sat in the audience, where attending crew sat.

When the table read got underway, it was a little disappointing. Some of the actors were much more mush-mouthed than they'd been in audition. Some even seemed like they were reading the script for the first time, with little or no feeling. Later, when I mentioned it to Roger, he told me not to worry about it because once the actors get into makeup and wardrobe and get on set, they feel much less self-conscious. Sitting at a table with no motion is not conducive to good acting. His advice was spot-on.

In the days following the reading, the focus was on the crew and their startup. All necessary crew came in that week to set the filming schedule, visit the locations for final set preparations, and to finalize a myriad of details. They met daily in our command center, which was a large room at the back of the Arts building. It had a huge mirror across the length of one wall, on which we posted the schedules for all the coming days of filming.

Bumps In The Road

Early on the morning of September 12th, the first real day of pre-production, I went to the store to buy food and drinks for breakfast and lunch for everyone. It was a totally mundane task and seemed like a waste of my time, given the list of duties awaiting me for the day. I was consumed with the managerial problems of the film, primarily those having to do with accounting. I was in over my head with taxes, payroll, and how to keep track of expenses. And I could see no way to get out of the bind I was already in. To be frank, I was very scared that I would fail.

I got to the command center early and set out the doughnuts and other items. Then I cornered Angel. "I am beside myself," I told him. "I simply cannot, cannot, cannot do the accounting properly. I need you to help me find a good accountant, if you can."

I explained that I had gotten Quickbooks set up, and indeed had been using it so far successfully. But I was not able to set up payroll correctly and I knew I simply wouldn't have the time to learn it. I also was very unsure of my ability to do the taxes right, especially unemployment and out-of-state taxes. I told Angel I had telephoned several accountants and hadn't found anyone with film experience who was available and affordable. And I didn't want to use an online system or someone who didn't know about film accounting.

As we talked in hushed tones, he glanced over to the food table where someone was reaching for a doughnut. Just as the man did so, he sneezed all over them. Angel quickly strode over and dumped all the two dozen doughnuts in the trash. Returning to me, he said, "That guy's two-year-old has a cold." I totally understood but wished the sneezer had been last in line instead of first.

Angel promised to work the problem immediately. He and Zubi looked that day for an accountant and came up with Harald Galinski, someone whom I'd already interviewed by phone. I had rejected him because he was way too expensive and was located in Austin. I wanted someone in Dallas with whom I could work directly.

Angel took command. He said he would talk to Harald about his fee and also see whether he could come to Dallas part-time. Ultimately, he got something worked out. When Harald came onto the production the next day, it was an enormous relief to me. If I were to have the film experience to do over again, one of the most important steps I'd take is to get the accountant before hiring almost anyone else.

Actors began arriving at the command center where they were going to meet each other and do three things: talk with the wardrobe people and go over any remaining questions they had about colors and sizes; get a session with our makeup artist so that she could make notes about skin color first-hand; and, for those in action scenes, work out with the stunt coordinator.

One of the actresses arrived with her two children, a girl of about four and a boy of two or three. The boy was visibly ill and had an awful gurgly cough. I told the actress that she needed to take him home right away or he might make others sick.

She surprised me greatly by not understanding how he might give the entire cast and crew whatever disease he had. Even more surprising to me was that she accused me of being a racist and told me that I was making her little boy feel like a pariah. I asked her to step outside to talk this through with me.

Outside, she raised her voice and became very combative, insisting that the only reason I wanted her to take the boy home was because she was black. I offered a mask to her and said he could stay if he wore it. She threw it on the ground.

I asked the wardrobe and makeup artists if they had any further need to talk to her. When they said no, the actress stormed away with her children. I wondered if I was going to have to find someone else to play her role. And I fervently hoped that no one would come down with whatever the child had.

Filming An Indie

The rest of the day was a blur to me, but I do recall that, as it came to a close, I reflected on the fact that I was not at all in tune with the cultural priorities and statuses in the film industry. The issues were all small, but they were a bit confusing to me. Let me give you just a couple of examples.

At the end of that first day there were a few condiments and leftovers that needed refrigeration. The kitchen was well away from our command center and I was shuttling things for quite a walk. I turned to the production designer and asked if she could help me carry some items over. She replied that I would have to get a production assistant (PA) to help me because that is in their job description, not hers. Oh, I thought to myself, this is one of those union requirements, so I'd better be careful whom I ask to do what.

I said, "OK," and picked up what I could, leaving only a few things I couldn't carry, and started out. She said, "I guess I can help you this time, but I won't do this again. Next time ask a PA."

Another "cultural" issue during pre-production, and throughout filming, is that I generally felt like a pariah. When I would walk in the room, no one would speak to me. If someone else walked in right behind me, they would be greeted. If I joined a conversation, it would stop. If I spoke to someone in the crew, the reply would be minimal. At one point, a young crew member asked me if I knew the answer to a question. Zubi pulled him aside as said that he was never, ever to ask me anything. If he were to have a question, he should only ask Zubi or his direct boss.

I asked Angel if I had done something to give myself the reputation as a dragon or a meanie. He said, "No, but you're the executive producer, and the screenwriter, and so on." And? I waited for him to explain. He just said that I wasn't exactly the foe, but I wasn't a friend either and never could be.

I didn't really get it, but I guessed that I didn't need to. I just needed to make things work out; I didn't need to be liked, loved, or included. My approach was to think of it like visiting a foreign country. People are basically alike deep down and are thus understandable on a human level. But the nuances of perspective and behavior that stem from cultural upbringing are hard to fathom as an outsider, so you just have to do what you can to learn what is culturally offensive and avoid doing it. But you can never really be culturally consonant if you are not *from* the culture.

Choreography Preparation

One of the most enjoyable days I had during preparations was when Roger and I met with Janell Smith, our stunt coordinator and action choreographer, in my apartment to discuss the final fight scene. Roger and I had some different views on how it should go, and we needed to reconcile those, but also make sure that Janell's expertise was fully exploited.

We began with a discussion of what the scene should accomplish. Roger said that although it is an action scene, there is information that needs to be inserted to give the audience some background. He felt we needed to insert dialog that conveyed a history between the two fighters.

I was strongly against adding dialog and argued that people don't discourse when there is a physical fight unto death. We settled on a compromise whereby the woman says, just before she bunts her forehead into her opponent's, "I should have killed you in Portland." I still think the line is contrived, but I was happy that he accepted there not being a longer conversation, and I think he was content with the line.

Janell was a creative expert throughout our meeting. We asked her how the blows could be exchanged with no one gaining the upper hand at first, and how the woman could overcome the bulk of her opponent. We went through the fight with Janell playing each person, showing us how it would look, and she made suggestions on how to gain credibility with the moves.

As we neared the end of our session, Janell asked how we wanted the fight to end, meaning how should Sarah kill Lehman. I said that I would like to use the same karate move that was used against a bad guy in the movie, *Billy Jack*. In that film, Billy uses his whole body to turn and build momentum, then, with his full arm extended, strikes his opponent's jugular with a knifehand chop (the outside of the hand from the little finger to the wrist). I thought it would be a move that a woman could execute well, even if she were wounded, and would be clearly fatal to the victim. Janell liked the idea and incorporated it.

Because we spent the time to prepare the scene, I think it turned out pretty well, certainly better than it would have been. It was filmed in the wee hours on the last day of shooting when everyone was exhausted. And, although there were some problems, I know for sure that the planning we did paid off.

Catering

The list of things I didn't know about making a movie is pretty long and for the most part not terribly interesting. But there are a few, in retrospect, that I think give a flavor of what a novice I was and how mundane some of the jobs that have to be done are.

Angel had told me we'd need a caterer to provide really good meals and snacks. He placed a high priority on making sure that people were well fed.

I called around, examined menus, and did telephone interviews. I picked one caterer and a back-up. But I didn't know what I was doing and didn't know that I didn't know.

What I was missing was a full appreciation of the hours of day in which breakfasts and lunches would be served, as well as the fact that they'd have to be delivered to wherever our set was. In retrospect, it seems obvious, but I didn't consider the fact that as we'd move through the filming schedule, the starts of the filming days would gradually become later and later, until our "day" would be starting at night. Thus, on our first day of filming breakfast would be at 5:00 AM and lunch at 11:00 AM. By the end of filming, breakfast would be served at 5:00 PM and lunch at 11:00 PM. So, we needed a caterer that would adjust to these highly varied mealtimes. And logistically, they would have to move all over town for delivery to wherever we were filming. The caterer I'd signed on would be able to do neither odd timing nor drive to many locations.

During pre-preproduction, after Angel learned of my mistake, he assigned someone else to start the search for a caterer all over. This person found an elderly couple willing to take on the odd-hours job and drive the meals to wherever we needed them. It amused me that the caterers I'd found, all of whom were young go-getters, said they wouldn't be up to the pressures of timing and location changes, whereas the old-timers—retired people with a start-up business and who looked to be in their late 70's—were ready and willing.

Although the couple said a contract wasn't needed, I wanted things in writing. Again, I can emphasize enough to any other inexperienced filmmaker—do contracts, put everything in writing. And keep your paper trail, including emails, until you are absolutely sure you will never, ever need them again. Here is an example of why.

Much later, on the last night of filming, after lunch was served around midnight, the caterers presented their second and final bill. I had already left a check with the agreed amount and "paid in full" written on it. But the final invoice the caterer presented contained a totally unexpected item for fuel consumed during deliveries—something we had agreed to not include in the contract. The production assistant told them I had already left the set for the night but had left the final check for them. They could either take it or leave it and present their case to me later. They took the check.

Security

Yet another early error is that I didn't think through the importance of security. We were renting many, many thousands of dollars' worth of equipment for lighting, sound, digital recording, communications, and sets. When we weren't shooting, these high-value items would be in trucks, which were themselves expensive and, obviously, mobile.

So, for 336 hours over the production period, this equipment would be unguarded, unless I were willing and able to pay either for them to be guarded or to place them in a secured facility somewhere, which would be grossly inconvenient, time-consuming for the back-and-forth, and impossibly expensive.

The issue of security hadn't really occurred to me until my insurance company called during the pre-production week and asked how the equipment would be stored during off-hours. They said that the insurance, even with the very high deductible, would not apply unless I could provide evidence that there were satisfactory safeguards in place.

I think that this is the kind of problem I was born to solve; it is like a managerial puzzle. There is an issue that seems to have no easy solution, but there is an answer, you just have to find it. So first look at the parameters: you can't hire a guard, therefore you need a guarded location; the location can't be far away; it has to be near to as many filming locations as possible; you don't have money to spend on the location, so it should be free. Ah ha! The police station!

I telephoned my contact in the Mesquite Police Department and asked if we could park our trucks in their fenced parking lot behind their building. The answer was no, due to insurance issues as well as the need to make sure that no one photographed police officers' private cars' license plates. But they had another idea almost as good: using the front parking lot in the "observed zone".

This zone is under continual observation by the police station's front desk via cameras surrounding a specific area of the parking lot. The original purpose of the zone is to provide a safe place where citizens can meet, for example, to sell items they've listed on Craig's List to a stranger and not get attacked or ripped off.

After sending the Mesquite Police photographs of the trucks and getting approval for their size, they agreed to allow our trucks to park in the zone whenever we wished during the two-week production. They would be brightly lit and under 24/7 police observation. It was perfect.

I called the insurance company back and got their approval too, so that the trucks and equipment would all be insured. To boot, the zone was less than a mile away from our command headquarters.

K. C. Bailey

Chapter 12: The First Week

At last the time had come to start filming. It was Saturday night and I sat quietly with Pono, wine in hand, thinking about it all. I was not sleeping well or for very long because of breathing problems, which was already taking a toll on me. And we hadn't really even begun.

As I meditated, I realized something very important: I had assembled the best talent I could afford and had a train ready to leave the station. All I had to do was climb aboard for a fantastic ride. It would be 20 days long, spread over four weeks. I needed to make sure that I enjoyed every hour of it. So, I was going to have to delegate as much as I could to others so that I could be witness to the birth of my film.

Pono climbed onto my lap and stared at me, purring. I felt her eyes conveyed a fey presence and knowledge. She made me feel like the small speck that I am, yet as important as anyone can be. I said aloud, "And I will be sure to take care of you." I imagined she replied, in Cat, "And I, you."

Day 1

I was fretting and pacing in the dark outside Belzie's Bar in a not-so-good part of town at 4:30 AM. I was alone in a rutted parking lot amid tromped Styrofoam cups, cigarette butts, and broken bottles. A neon sign cast pale yellow light. The night air, calm and cool, contrasted with the roiling sense of heat inside me. I was really, really on edge. What if no one showed up to open the bar? And what could I do if they didn't? Even though I'd tried, they had declined giving me a key or working out a backup plan. How could I have let there be no backup plan?

Filming An Indie

As I berated myself, the equipment truck pulled up. My heart soared as I realized that now my filming was to begin. I stared at Belzie's door, willing it to open. And it did. Elation!

I walked inside and was surprised to find there were three people already there, one behind the bar and two seated at it. But I didn't recognize anyone. Neither the owner, his manager, nor any of the bar personnel I had previously met were present.

One guy was having a drink already. I went to speak to him, and he told me he was the new owner. I gulped hard, wondering how on earth there could be a new owner in less than 48 hours after I had got the "old" owner to sign a Location Agreement.

I slid onto the bar stool next to him and began to chat him up about signing a Location Agreement. And I was wondering whether I would have to pay a second location fee, as the first fee had already been paid to the "first owner."

After I had got agreement to sign from the second owner, the first owner arrived. He sat at the other end of the bar, ordered a drink, and was glowering at the new owner. Now I was really confused, to say the least. Here I had two owners, who obviously were at odds with one another, and I needed to sort out who the legal one was.

Around us was a swirl of activity as the crew brought in equipment and materials. Metal clanged, heavy furniture scraped across the floors, people shouted orders. The set dressing began immediately, and the hum of activity was fascinating. I wanted to sit on the sidelines and enjoy the process, but the ownership problem demanded solving.

Then the first owner's manager came in. I took her aside and quietly asked her, "Who's the real owner?"

She explained that the bar had been sold to pay a debt between the two and the closing of the sale wouldn't take place until the next day, Monday, so I was still okay with the first Location Agreement. She went on to say that the two men were enemies and would best be kept apart.

Oh, great, I thought, just what we need—two guys who hate each other drinking at 5:00 AM in the middle of our first set on the first day. They were still sitting there sipping their alcohol, glaring at one another like two aging roosters, neither of which could claim his territory. I needed to be on good terms with both, so I went from one to the other casually, chatting a bit about what was going on, hoping to put them in good moods.

There was a change in pitch of the hubbub behind me. I turned and saw the cast and crew getting breakfast that had been delivered by the caterer. I was impressed at how quickly the elderly couple set things up.

Some of the crew wolfed their breakfasts and got busy placing gels over lights. The set decorators didn't even stop to eat; they were still removing excess paraphernalia. Nothing could be done about some of the junk in the room, like a refrigerator near the pool table. There hadn't been much time for the production designer and art department to prepare, given the quick change of venues for the bar scene. I felt sorry for them that their first day had been made hectic by the location problems, but I was impressed at how adaptable they were.

I watched Roger preparing for the filming. He was studying the pool table and talking with the cinematographer about how to capture an opening scene. I enjoyed the discussion and told myself, "Now this is what I am doing this all for!"

When the scene was finally done, I was even more impressed with the result on film. I absolutely loved the shot that became the opening for the scene. It was of the bad guy, leaning over the pool table, cue in hand, then breaking the balls.

Filming at this scene took way too long for a variety of reasons. One was that a key actor in the scene showed up late, unshaven, and mistake prone. He looked and acted hung over. Someone had to rush out to find shaving materials, which necessitated finding an open drugstore at 7:00 AM.

Once we had him shaved and got the filming underway, he kept making little mistakes that messed up the scene takes. For example, he kept bumping his head into the light over the pool table. Then he broke the balls in a way that looked like he'd never held a cue before. Then he broke the beer bottle during a practice run, when he wasn't supposed to. (This mattered because we'd brought only a few of the bottles that you use in filming—ones that are made of sugar and won't hurt anyone when you smash them.) Meanwhile, the struggles unnerved the co-actor in the scene, who began to flub his lines. Roger had to shoot the pool table scene over, and over, and over.

It was nearing noon when suddenly bar patrons started coming in, which not only messed up the lighting with sunlight every time the door opened but also caused noise and disruption. No one was supposed to be allowed in until 2:00 PM, when Belzie's Sunday hours began, according to our Location Agreement. I needed to fix the problem, so I went to ask the (still drinking) owners what was going on.

I learned that the new owner had decided that he would change the Sunday hours from opening at 2:00 PM to opening at noon to allow patrons to see the Cowboys' game on TV. He had advertised the new schedule all during the previous week. Great, I thought, I wonder if I am going to encounter surprises akin to this on every location.

We were nearing a wrap on this scene, so I negotiated for them to keep the TV on mute another 45 minutes. I told Roger we had to put it in high gear, as we needed to get out and get on with the next location anyway.

As we left Belzie's, I was so very glad the scene was done and fervently hoped that no other locations would be as problematic. More importantly, I was grateful that I had got a backup for the bar. I vowed that from now on, I would try even harder to have a verified backup for every location and that I would check the ownership question more carefully. I know big-budget movies have this all down pat, but it was really hard for my low-budget indie (being put together by a know-nothing newbie like me) to nail it.

We picked up and moved about 10 miles away to the next location, a gun shop named The Armory. It was owned by a very gentlemanly man, Darin Peterson. I had paid him not only the location use fee, but also a separate sum for being the movie's firearms consultant. I had been hesitant about the latter, but Angel had been insistent, which turned out to be a very good thing to do. (This exemplified why Angel was absolutely essential to the filming success and to making sure we did so many things correctly.)

I had no concept of the amount of work that Darin would have to do in preparation. He devoted an entire day to checking and clearing (of possible ammunition) every firearm in the shop. And that was *a lot* of firearms. And, of course, he had to be present as oversight for the entire time because we were near the weapons and ammunition.

The gun shop was a much smaller space than the bar had been, so I squeezed myself behind a gun display case on the side of the room to watch. The room quickly became hot and seemingly airless with 40 people breathing and our having had to turn off the air-conditioning to mute it.

Filming the gun shop scene was a pretty frustrating process to observe. It seemed that each take was exactly the same, with no change in the pace, angle, or action from each one to the next. It turned out that we spent 5 hours to get the one scene, which in the movie is pretty short.

Later, during editing, I would realize that there were two ways that the scene could be presented: one that would emphasize the girl's fear and anguish; the other would play up the gun shop owner's sorrow at not being able to help her. As the script was written, the former was the focus. But it seemed to me that what had been filmed, and the best cinematography, was on the latter. It was a challenge to cut and paste the pieces together to get the center of the scene to be on the girl.

At last Day 1 was finished and I left as the crew began to pack up. I therefore missed the hoopla about the equipment truck.

We had rented a large truck with a very comprehensive and extremely expensive set of lighting and other equipment. The rental company told us that there'd been battery issues with the truck, but that now they were fixed. But they weren't and the truck wouldn't start.

Angel, at the end of a 12-hour day, was faced with the problem that the truck was in a bad neighborhood, had no protection, and couldn't be moved. He had to stay with the truck for hours until someone could come and jump it. Then he had to get it to the police station late at night, which was a tiring ordeal. This was but one of the many times that Angel had to handle an unforeseen mishap.

In retrospect, I should have had in my contract with the equipment company that the truck would be in perfect mechanical condition and that if any problems occurred, they would immediately provide a replacement. As it was, it took days to get the truck battery replaced so we could trust it to start.

Day 2

I mentioned earlier that I had known about the Mesquite Arts Center because I was having a show of my photography there. I had hoped that the show would coincide with the filming so that my photography could be the backdrop for a scene in which the lead actors discuss their criminal cases. It worked out, and that scene was first up for filming on day two of production.

This scene was the first time that the "one director" conversation between Roger and me had an impact on my behavior during filming. Five extras had shown up to be in the movie. Roger sat two women at a table in the background, had one do a shadow crossing at the outset of the scene, and the two males walk in the far background.

Roger was watching the filming of the first take from the sidelines, not in the Video Village where I was. (The Video Village is where a monitor is set up to show what the film looks like as it is being shot so that you will know exactly how it will look to the audience.)

From Roger's perspective, he couldn't see two things. One was that the two lead actors in the scene were totally blocking the view of the seated women, thus negating their value as "populating" the scene. Second, the shadow woman was unrecognizable and so fleeting that she could be used as someone walking through the background to make it look less empty.

I got up after take one and stood near the sidelines to try to communicate the problems. When Roger and I made eye contact, I subtly as I could motioned to him. He "replied" by holding his hand up and looking away, signaling a message that I read as, "Don't bother me, I'm directing." I returned to my seat in the Video Village.

When the second take was shot and the same problems persisted, I contemplated just walking out and whispering to him, but the one-director talk was fresh in my mind. I decided on a different approach.

I motioned to the First Assistant Director, Michelle Millette, and told her that the two women needed to be moved to stage right in order to be visible in the scene. (I decided not to address the waste of the extra whose shadow was being used.) Michelle said nothing but walked back on set and moved the women. Roger asked her what she was doing, and she told him simply that she was moving the women. He told her, "I'm the director here," but he didn't move them back. To her credit, Michelle neither mentioned me nor looked my way.

The third take worked well, and the two women could be seen clearly. But another problem started to bug me. Why would the detectives be wearing their service weapons and badges when they're at an art gallery on their day off? (It was their day off; otherwise they could not logically be in an art gallery.) Again, I wanted to consult Roger, but I kept quiet because filming was already underway, and it would be too time-consuming to start the entire process of filming this scene over.

As I watched, I began kicking myself for not writing instructions about their attire and props in the script. I'd purposely avoided doing so because all the screenwriting textbooks on the subject say that such minutiae shouldn't be in a script. Clearly, in this case, it should have been.

I would not realize a third problem with the scene—and one that would plague other scenes as well—until I was later editing the film: there was no B roll. (B roll is footage shot that can be inserted during editing to help the spacing of the film and to add to the audience's knowledge about the location, mood, and/or time of day.) For example, it would have been highly useful to have had a zoom in on the picture that the two characters are discussing so that the audience could clearly see what they are talking about.

For the afternoon's shooting, we moved to the art studio of Rebecca Boatman, the location for the lead detective's pottery studio. (Rebecca was also the artist who sculpted the bust of Nyx for the movie.) I was anxious about this scene because it was the first time that the lead actors, Chad and Sasha, would romantically interact and kiss. So far, the two actors had been pretty aloof from one another on set and off, so I was a bit worried that they'd be stilted.

As I was getting ready to leave the morning's location to drive across town, I had an unforeseen opportunity. Our cinematographer. Terra Gutmann-Gonzalez needed a ride, so I took her along with me. As we rode, she asked me how I envisioned the one and only love scene that was to take place in a bedroom. Even though that filming was several days away, I was delighted she was already thinking about it.

I told her I thought the scene should be filmed from above, like the famous shot of John Lennon and Yoko Ono in bed. And, although I knew instinctively that our female star would not go along with showing much skin, I wanted at least a shot of her upper back as she got out of bed at the end of the scene.
Terra didn't reply, so I was unsure what she thought about my ideas. But later I would be ever so pleased we'd had this conversation.

At the shoot of the art studio scenes, I was able to watch only a little of the filming because I kept being called away for managerial things. One of the odd ones I dealt with that day was the issue of muscle cars.

Budget woes were a pervasive presence in my head throughout the movie-making process, almost like a fug of fear clouding my judgment. I expected some unforeseen expense cropping up that would end the whole enterprise because there were no deep pockets and no financier to turn to. So, I watched expenditures closely every day. But it wasn't just a few sudden big-ticket items that unexpectedly came up, it was also the pile up of little stuff.

One of the problems was that others on the team had the sense that this was a better-financed movie—like a studio production—than it was, so they tended to be cavalier about spending. I knew, for example, that some of the people whose gasoline I had to pay for in order for them to do their jobs were cheating. And the wastefulness in the meals, drinks and snacks thrown away was unnerving. But I couldn't afford the time and energy to solve these little problems in real time. I had to watch for difficulties with more costly issues. An example was muscle cars.

I noticed on Day 2 that one of the management team was spending a lot of time looking at images of cars on the computer. I had no idea what he was doing and was irritated at his wasting time this way. Before I could say anything to him, I was called away to handle some problem and forgot about it.

A few hours later, he came to me with some printouts of photos of three cars. He explained that he and a couple of other members of the team had selected these cars as "picture cars"—cars to rent for use in the movie. These flashy vehicles would cost several hundred dollars a day and would be required for multiple days. They definitely were not in the budget. I took him aside and told him that under no circumstances were we going to rent muscle cars. I was really surprised when he pushed back, saying that we needed to have cars that matched the personalities of the two cops and the woman who was stalked.

I decided that discussion was pointless. For some reason, he just didn't have a true grip on budgetary constraints. I told him very firmly, tamping anger that was creeping into my voice, that there would be absolutely no more discussion of the issue. I had arranged to borrow friends' cars for the film and that was that.

Over and over money was an issue. It was lonely sometimes making the calls on where to spend. I wished I could have done a better job not only keeping waste down, but also conveying the limits of my finances to the management team. There just wasn't the time; we had been assembled too quickly to allow for team building and development of shared vision and values.

At the end of Day 2, when I reviewed the takes of the studio scene, I was particularly happy with the last one, after Sasha had some practice with the kiss part. She comes across as shy rather than cold. And I was especially pleased with the ad-libbing (something I usually don't like, as it can mess up sequencing in edits). Chad had taken aside the artist, Rebecca Boatman, and asked her about pottery—questions such as how hot the kilns got and how clay behaves. He then sprinkled his lines with this information, adding tremendously to the credibility of his role.

Looking back with 20/20 hindsight, I see three problems in shooting at this location that would persist throughout the filming. My inexperience prevented me from recognizing them at the time. The first, which I have already mentioned, was the lack of B roll filming. In this case, we did no B roll showing the two professional kilns at the studio. Those kilns were one of the primary reasons I so much wanted Rebecca Boatman's studio for the film. Unfortunately, there was not one single shot of them. Had they been included it would have added tremendously to the credibility of the location. As it is, the viewer might readily assume that we just pretended that a location was an artist's studio.

The second was not identifying at the time of shooting that the film was not being properly exposed. Almost any time we shot outside, or had natural light in the background, this became an issue. Later, during coloring, we were able to correct for some of this, but there are several shots that are integral to the film, but which are substandard because of exposure. One of these unsolvable exposure problems was at the art studio.

The third was a plague: the camera was very, very often out of focus. Later my editor, Charles Willis, and I would end up choosing several less preferred takes simply because they were more in focus.

After the artist studio scene, which went very smoothly, the team left for the third location of the day—the Corinthian Sailing Club on White Rock Lake. Originally, I planned just to have the scene be on the shore of the lake. Angel didn't say anything about that but was apparently hoping for a place with more visual richness. He found one.

Angel kept his search within the parameter he knew I most wanted for the mood of the scene—the lake. He had found the sailing club and accidentally encountered the man in charge there, a real character nicknamed "Red Dog," who later signed a Location Agreement with me via email.

One scene shot at the Corinthian Club features the two lead characters having a philosophical conversation. An interesting problem cropped up which, thankfully, didn't happen often: the lines were not spoken precisely as scripted in any of the takes but one. This had two effects.

There is a line that goes, "I figure I am like a dog. A dog can understand some of what we say to it, but it can never speak our language. The answers to the big questions are as far beyond me as speaking English is to a dog."

In all of the takes of the scene except one, the word "is" is omitted, which could make the sentence meaning change from "Speaking English is beyond the capacity of the dog" to "Speaking English to a dog is beyond me." Admittedly the latter interpretation would be odd, and this is the lesser problem. But it led to a bigger issue.

During editing, I wanted to use the one take in which the line was correctly spoken. But to do so meant using the same take for other cut shots in the scene because using any other take would entail footage that had a slightly different angle, lighting, and positions of the actors. If the exact same words had been spoken in all of the takes, we would have been able to use better clips and edit for close ups on the actress.

One of the most fantastic outcomes of Angel's coup in getting us the Corinthian Club location was an exceptional wordless scene. Roger had a stroke of brilliance in filming the lead detective, played by Chad Halbrook, in his solitary torment. Chad and Roger achieved just the right mix of simmering anger and, at the end, harsh resolve. I also like the scene because it was long enough to feature some music. There are too few places in the movie that "breathe" and allow for the mood to be set by music, but this scene was one.

It was interesting and instructive to me that later this wordless scene would elicit radically different reactions from the preliminary reviewers from whom we sought early feedback. They ranged from "delete this worthless scene" to "wow, this is a very effective moment…good job!". These wildly differing responses taught me to take any of the "professional" film expert's assessments with a grain of salt. There is no one right answer in film because it is art.

Day 3

Obtaining permission to film in the Mesquite Police Department (MPD) gym was a stroke of good fortune because it is ultra-modern with a blue-hued light and has state-of-the-art equipment. As part of our agreement with MPD, we were to have only a few hours there. Not only did they want to quickly return the gym to its purpose in time for officers coming off the next shift, they had to dedicate an officer to baby-sit us because we were inside of the secure area where the public was not allowed unescorted.

I hadn't appreciated what an ordeal it would be to change the gym around to make it into a set. The large, heavy exercise machines had to be moved mostly to one side of the room, which took not only brawn, but time. We had to carefully photograph each piece of equipment before moving it so that it could be replaced precisely after we had finished. Then another issue arose: lighting.

The crew wanted to delay filming until they could cover up the windows to omit the blue-hued light. I met Roger in the hallway and quietly told him that the delay was unacceptable for two reasons. First, we were on a timer agreed to with the police that couldn't be changed, and we were already chewing up a lot of time moving equipment around. Second, to remove the hue was to destroy some of the elegance of the set. The light color was one of the reasons Angel and I had chosen this gym over the half dozen others we had considered. Roger agreed and went to talk to the cinematographer.

Unfortunately, she reversed Roger's resolve. She convinced him that changing the lighting (covering the large windows, shielding the overhead lights, and setting up new lights) would take less than 30 minutes and if it were not better, then we could revert. So, Roger agreed, thinking that he was compromising between what I wanted and what the crew wanted. But that was not the case: he was agreeing to a significant delay that would result in an unusable set.

It took more than an hour for the crew to make the proposed lighting changes and it made the scene look dark. What was worse is that the lighting was now florescent rather than natural. Roger and I again met in the hallway and I told him that I was very, very unhappy. He said he was also. He went and told the crew to go back to the original lighting. By then, our schedule was so far behind we never recouped.

While the crew was changing the lighting back to the blue-hued natural state of the room, I noticed that the lead actor, Chad Halbrook, was doing chin-ups in the corner of the room. Rather than communicating with him directly that I didn't want him wasting his energy that way, I sought out Roger. "Roger, Chad is using energy I think he should save for all the takes he is going to do where he has to press weights." Roger told me not to worry, that Chad would be fine.

I wondered to myself whether I was over-reacting. Maybe I shouldn't fret so much. Maybe I should just relax and let the director direct. Then my little niggling muse snickered, "Yeah, but it's your one and only film and nobody else will care about the details like you will. Go tell Roger to stop Chad *now*." But I didn't, and later regretted it because his exhaustion had an outsized impact on the film, about which I will tell you more later.

I was able to watch only some of the filming in the gym because I had an errand to attend to. Thus, I was not present when the crew had to hurry the filming because they were running out of time. I will never know if the rush is what led to further mistakes on this location or not, but I would learn later during editing that the fabulous location of the gym was for naught, which I will explain later.

My errand was to go and get an ancient white pickup truck from my brother-in-law. He had agreed to our using it as the vehicle for the villain, George Lehman. Although we had a driver and car for the production, he was busy this day and unable to take my in-law home after he delivered the truck to my apartment. I had to be ready to do all kinds of jobs.

Although I had intended to get the truck, give Pono her insulin and food, and then return to set to see evening filming at the MPD, a new problem confronted me. Permission to use location for filming a scene the next week was being pulled.

The location—the Training Room of the Mesquite Civic Building—had been a great coup. It is a gorgeous venue of glass and steel with wonderful natural light. We'd had to agree to use it during business hours, which was going to be a logistics problem with the public being present, but it was worth the hassle.

We were due to film at the Training Room on a Monday but received word on Friday that the Mesquite City Council had decided unexpectedly that they would meet in that room on Monday so we would be bumped. I nearly had a meltdown, but Carol, our point-of-contact with Mesquite, came to the rescue. She offered to come in on

Sunday to allow us to film. We accepted. Angel hurriedly reworked the film schedule with First Assistant Director Michelle Millette and Second AD Rudy Gutierrez. (Each numbered Assistant Director has its own specific duties and expertise.)

Jumping ahead a bit, let me add here that the change turned out to be a superb stroke of luck. While it caused us to rework the filming schedule and logistics, we had the building to ourselves. We didn't have to worry about people walking onto our scene or uncontrollable noises messing up our audio. Providing the building to us on Sunday was just one example of the above-and-beyond attitude of Carol and the City of Mesquite.

That night I sat thinking with my wine in hand about Angel and how our partnership was evolving. We are such different people that we unlikely would have given each other a moment's notice under normal circumstances. Yet here we were almost in a sort of marriage, working on divvying up responsibilities and trying to make an enormous undertaking work. And in one very big respect, his task was more onerous than mine: he was trying to teach me various jobs and to help make sure I did them right, yet also working to make sure that my experience of the filmmaking was as rewarding as possible.

During those moments that night was probably the first time I realized that I was beginning to love Angel. I knew that my feelings for him were now deep respect and admiration. And I felt my loyalty to him growing.

Day 4

The first thing I did when I got to the Art Center where we were starting our work on Day 4 was to go and check with Laurel Goetz Warren, our Digital Imaging Technician. She is a kind and reserved person who worked very, very hard to do as close to a perfect job as she could. She welcomed me with her ever-beautiful smile.

As we reviewed some of the takes from the previous night taken in the MPD parking lot, my happy demeanor drained away. What I saw was a big wardrobe mistake.

Detective Coxon is a character who prides himself on his attire and prefers to wear jacket and tie. He isn't in the least sloppy. Despite this being clear throughout the script and in all discussion about his wardrobe, Coxon was dressed in a shirt that was way too large. You could put your entire hand between his neck and shirt collar. I was very upset and wanted the scene re-shot.

Angel took me aside and pointed out that the entire schedule would slip dramatically if we did a re-shoot and that we would mess up the logistics for all the locations, including the Airbnbs we had rented. It was a convincing argument; we could not alter the production schedule for a single wardrobe error, regardless of how noticeable it was. I backed down.

I put the wardrobe question behind me for the moment and turned my attention to the day's agenda. We were shooting outside with a borrowed truck for the bad guy and, most importantly, a very expensive Dallas Area Rapid Transit bus rented with a paid driver for the scene.

Although we had submitted the filming sequence weeks before so that the City of Mesquite and MPD would know about it, there were no MPD blockades for the street on which we were filming. I should have asked for that specifically instead of just expecting it to happen. Because I hadn't, kids on bikes decided it would be fun to crash the film. They kept going back and forth, messing up the scene. They were a distraction and were costing money and time. But no one, neither the crew nor Roger, made any move to resolve the problem, so I stepped in.

I called MPD to let them know I'd like some barricades to help keep people out. Instead, they sent a very bored officer who sauntered onto the street where we were trying to film. The crew went silent and all action stopped while I went out to talk to him. After I'd explained about the kids, he waved his arm to shoo them away. They rode off, but I had no confidence they wouldn't return after he'd left. He promised he'd come back with barricades as he went back to his squad car, but he never did. But the kids didn't come back either and we were able to get on with filming.

Because our shooting day started at 1:00 PM, I had to leave after only a few hours to go and do Pono's insulin. As I left the set, I turned on my phone. All kinds of small managerial issues were demanding my attention—phone calls to return, emails to send, papers to process, and details to attend.

Filming An Indie

The worst of the long list of problems was budgetary. While it was a perpetual problem that there wasn't enough money to do what we'd like to do, the issue at-hand was urgent—locking the budget.

A movie budget is supposed to be locked before production even begins. But Angel hadn't been ready to do that and would not agree to our accountant Harald's insistence that we make a firm decision. Here it was, Day 4, and Harald was telling me that he could not go on working on a movie without a locked budget. He told me he would quit if it were not resolved. I spoke at length with him, asking for another day to work on Angel to get it nailed down. He agreed to another day, but only one more or he'd quit.

After doing Pono's insulin, I returned to the filming after dark. I didn't want to miss seeing the hospital scenes shot. I had spent perhaps more effort on securing that location than any other and I was eager to see for myself how it would play out.

I don't know if my sensitivities were off or there was indeed a bad vibe on set. It seemed that everyone was a bit on edge. I told myself that it was probably just me, with the conversation on the budget with Harald and other things pressing on me. However, I did note that the filming preparations looked more disorganized than usual and it was taking much longer to get the camera rolling. In fact, when the crew broke for lunch at almost 9:00 PM, nothing had been shot.

I decided to leave because my physical state was plummeting. The cramps in my feet and legs were excruciating and I felt I could not stand for more than a few minutes.

As I walked out of the hospital, I saw 5 young women sitting in the back lobby, the one unused by the hospital near where we were filming. I asked if they were extras and they excitedly affirmed they were, seemingly happy that someone had finally recognized them. I asked if anyone had come to talk to them yet about what they were to do, and they said no.

I went back and found a production assistant and told her to show the extras to the food, get their information, and to make sure that they were used in the film. After all, they were showing up late on a Wednesday night just to be in the movie; they should be rewarded. I then left.

Later, I was very sad to learn that they'd never been used and that after waiting for hours, they had finally left. I have kicked myself so many times since for not making sure extras were better treated.

When finally I got home that night and opened the evening wine, I welcomed it with relief from the minutia that I so wished I could delegate to someone else. I drank wine until I could safely tell myself that I was in absolutely no condition to make any decision or do any work; being drunk was freedom.

That night in bed, I felt very weak and struggled for breath, waking minutes after any moment I fell asleep, gasping. I was sitting up in bed, propped by pillows. I thought about how breathing had once been without thought; now my breathing was so shallow I had to consciously take deeper breaths. I was afraid of falling soundly asleep. I wasn't being melodramatic when I wondered if I would see the next dawn, let alone the film being finished. I resolved in the night to call my close friend Aman in the morning to get him to co-sign on my Pono Productions bank account and to promise to see the film finished if I were to die.

At 3:00 AM my mood was extremely bleak. The cramps were intermittent but severe and breathing was a struggle. For the first time, I felt more tired and ready for death than I felt afraid of the end. Truly, I feel the only thing that kept me going through that night was the sleeping kitty on the pillow beside me. I kept worrying about who would feed her and give her insulin. I was able to get up at 4:30 AM and test her blood, give her insulin, and feed her, but it was with extreme effort.

Day 5

As I watched the sun rise, I could barely move. It wasn't just a matter of very little sleep. My muscles were weak. My hands seemed not to want to respond to my mental commands and, when they did, it was a millisecond late. It was weird, like I was out of synch or in some time-lapse.

I lay there thinking; I badly wanted to go and watch the filming. It was the first day that the Woman In Black was supposed to be in a scene, and a very important scene. In it, the woman unleashes her rage against the rapist, whom she has cornered. He reveals his misogynist hatred. The dialog is heated and laden, requiring the utmost skill from the actress particularly. Her motives and raw emotions are laid bare. It would be exciting to see the one of the most emotional scenes in the movie filmed.

But I also wanted to go because I was worried about the Woman In Black's costume. Roger had made an offhand comment about a ninja outfit and I wanted to make sure that whatever he meant didn't look silly and cartoonish. I had wanted to discuss it with him the day before but never seemed to get to it.

Also, I had been concerned by the makeup artist's erratic approach to the lead actress's eye makeup and vampy hair. I'd wanted to talk to Roger about that too. I thought about calling him, but I didn't want to disturb him in case he was still asleep. He was already showing signs of exhaustion and I wanted him as fresh as he could be when the filming started that afternoon.

I tried to get out of bed, but my body wouldn't cooperate. I was too weak to rise. But I really needed to go to the toilet and was afraid of wetting the bed if I didn't do it soon.

I slid my legs over the side and twisted onto my stomach at the edge of the bed, dropping to my knees. With my knees on the floor and arms on the bed, I pushed myself up slowly to stand, but with my weight still on my hands on the bed.

Just standing was a lengthy ordeal and I was panting like I'd just run. When finally I stood, I slowly plodded to the bathroom. My gait seemed off and I felt it a strain to walk straight.

Getting onto the toilet was more a fall than a sit. Then I struggled to rise. I had to repeat what I'd done to get out of bed. It occurred to me that this was my last day. I tried to think of what to do about Pono. When I made it back to bed, I was at a point that I wasn't even thinking about the film anymore. I was trying to plan my last day alive and whom to call, what to do.

I finally fell asleep for a while. I awoke feeling better and breathing easier. It was still shallow, and I was working for every breath, but my hands were better. And, I was able to get out of bed without the ordeal of the early morning. I inched my way to my computer to check to see if there were any messages about the film, as we were supposed to start the day in a couple of hours.

An email had come in from the Mesquite Arts Center management. It suggested that our access to the building might be restricted and that we might need to be escorted to parts of the building. I was shocked. If this were to happen, we would no longer be able to work and film there, as our hours were not normal, and we were using several areas of the complex for scenes. I wondered what on earth had prompted this. Then I saw there were two documents attached to the email. They were from one of the building's regular users, the Mesquite Community Theater (presumably fellow artists). These documents explained why we were possibly going to be restricted.

The community theater was protesting our use of the building. They objected to our invading "their" space and made a number of unfounded claims, including that we were using their props without permission and interrupting their rehearsals. I knew neither was true. They sought to get the management to either restrict the areas of the building where we could film and the times we could operate or simply oust us altogether.

In a way, I wasn't surprised at the accusations. The leadership of the community theater had made remarks that showed their envy about the moviemaking and jealousy about our use of space that normally they used exclusively. But the threat implicit in the Arts Center management forwarding the letters, instead of themselves dealing with them and backing us up, was very serious.

I knew had to respond in order to assure we continued to have approval for using the location. We had already scheduled almost one-fifth of the filming to take place in the Arts Center and were using a big room there as our operations hub. The cast and crew consisted of dozens of people and to escort them around would be an onerous, if not impossible, task. If we were put out of the building, it would be the end of the film. I had no backup for this multi-use location.

Surely I could refute their claims about interfering with their work, but I also needed to do it in a diplomatic enough way to convince the Arts Center management that we were cooperative and not at fault. I struggled to contain my anger at the pettiness of the charges, at the utter waste of time it was for me to address this, and at the lack of spine by the Arts Center management in not dealing with it instead of lobbing it into my lap. I set aside the email for a bit to collect my thoughts and let my anger ebb. The emotion of it all made me feel even weaker.

I turned to some other issues: I needed to get some insurance certificates for locations uses; there were three contracts to fill out and get signed; a crew member was trying to cheat on his hours submitted for pay that I had to refute; our accountant needed some input for his numbers on Texas tax payments; there were three non-disclosure agreements to get signed; a crew member was posting on social media despite a prohibition against that and I needed to fix it; and, there were problems with some timesheets Angel had erroneously approved.

And then came the worst emails. I was getting information from Harald, my accountant, about paychecks to be written. Everyone would be waiting to be paid the next morning, so I needed to do the checks today. I had known it was coming, but I hadn't imagined it would coincide with so many other pressing issues.

I laid my head on my desk, wishing I could be anywhere else. I thought of the filming to get underway soon. I imagined myself deleting all the emails and ignoring all the to-dos. I could then just go and watch, with no obligations. But that was a daydream. It seemed that my hope of having a thrill ride making a movie was turning into a morass of managerial tasks. Slowly, I got out the checks and brought the information up on the screen about who was to receive how much. I then tried to write checks.

I couldn't write. I would mentally say the name of the person to fill in on the check and it would come out a jerky squiggle with letters missing. It was as if I had some sort of palsy. How could I skip letters when writing a name? This had never happened before.

Instead of seconds to write a check, it took minutes. I had to speak aloud each letter and numeral so that I wouldn't skip anything. Just writing a few checks was a horrible ordeal. And it looked like someone who'd never written in English before; my handwriting looked nothing like my own. I would pause, looking at the long list of remaining names, wishing I had someone to call to come and write for me.

Midway through, I had a meltdown. My right hand simply would write no more. And I mean physically—my hand would not respond to my brain's commands. My fingers and palm were cramping. Never before had my hands cramped, only my feet and lower legs.

I began to weep. I wasn't just sorry for myself, although there was that. I was scared now that I'd started something I couldn't finish and that everyone depending on me would be disappointed and more. Actors with families to support had taken time off of work to be in *my* film. They were counting on these checks—checks I couldn't physically write—to make it worth their while.

After sobbing for a while, I started again. It took so inordinately long, requiring many rest stops. After hours more than it should have taken, I finished the checks.

I rested my head on the desk for a bit and then turned to typing the rebuttal email that I hoped would save our use of the Arts Center. My right hand was exhausted from the check writing, so I mostly pecked with my left, using my right only to make capital letters. What a dark, dark day it was for me. Although I was able to finish the most urgent of tasks that had piled up, I didn't get to watch any of the filming that day. I just went back to bed as soon as I could.

Weekend 1

We had Friday and Saturday off, which meant time for me to catch up on the list of bureaucratic things I hadn't been able to finish. I was feeling much stronger and breathing better, so I began work early in the morning.

First up was the problem of the wardrobes of the lead actors. I had not yet sorted out the solution to the ill-fitting clothes. I had already told Roger about my being upset and he was well aware that I had even wanted to re-shoot the scene that had Chad wearing a huge-collared shirt. Yet, when I asked our Wardrobe Director, Jamie Puente, if anything had been done to resolve it, she said no. Rather than bothering Roger about it, or risk waking him when I knew he needed rest, I decided to work the issue myself.

In a few telephone calls and email exchanges, Jamie and I worked on what to do about the shirts, the colors, and the need to get some better jackets for the remaining un-shot days. We also addressed the other two detectives' wardrobes. I told her to make sure that Sam Kang, who wore Aloha shirts, would never wear a tee shirt underneath, and that Detective Raul Garcia be only in dark-toned tee shirts. We discussed the type of shirt needed to fit each character. The differences would help accentuate their personalities.

Jamie and I also discussed the costume and makeup of the Woman in Black. On this, there was a total miscommunication by me with the staff. The Woman was supposed to be in a ski mask because this character would be trying to keep her hair from leaving forensic evidence, not because she was attempting to be some ninja. With a ski mask on, she would need no heavy black makeup. It would just make her look silly. But, indeed, the actress was told to wear a hoodie that made her look like a Darth-Vader wannabe and had ridiculously black eyes. It was one of the several reasons that the scene is almost non-existent in the film. Only the shots of her required for the integrity of the story were left in, and with cuts that minimize views of the Woman In Black.

Although Jamie and I resolved some problems with wardrobe, others would only become clear to me only in the editing phase. Here is an example.

One wonderful section of film that had to be cut due to wardrobe problems was one in which the two lead detectives walk down a hallway talking about relationships. The lighting was magnificent, and the architecture of the hallway had great production value. The cinematographer did a masterful job of starting the scene with their feet, then working up their bodies as they walked.

The problem was that Coxon's pants were about 4 inches too long, bunched up at his ankles, looking sloppy and out-of-character. I don't think anyone anticipated that the shot would include their feet and thus they didn't think about the pants.

In addition to talking to Jamie about wardrobe that weekend, I also needed to work with Angel and Harald on the budget. Angel was now ready to pull the trigger on locking it. I let Harald know and told him we absolutely needed him, even if we tried his patience. The three of us met in my apartment and agreed on the final numbers. It took about three hours to hammer it out, moving monies from one account to another to try to figure out how we should allocate the remaining funds.

The weekend was also time to catch up with Angel. We were always running in different directions, although we were in contact almost continuously via email and text. He was working on a couple of last-minute hires. An actor and actress had unexpectedly dropped out and he and I hustled to look at Roger's audition videos to pick a backup. I had already organized the backups in order of priority, based on the evaluation sheets and Roger's and my previous consultations, so we were able to sign on the next most preferred talent.

One of the things that Angel brought me up to date on was disturbing. The actor who played the villain Bruce Brown (Tony Herbert) had been made up as a dead body on Day 5. The makeup artist had used some sort of dark material on him that didn't wash off easily. He'd had to shower and scrub himself almost raw to try to remove it. He was mighty unhappy about it. Angel said that we have to insist that the makeup be professional grade and be done properly. I agreed and he said he'd speak to the makeup artist about it.

I finished up my weekend work by resolving the issue with the Community Theater and assuring our ability to continue using the Arts Center. I gave the management a letter that refuted successfully all claims and assured we would keep our privileges in the building. Dealing with envy surely can be a waste of time.

When evening came, I sat with my cat and wine, wishing I could talk with Angel. He had moved out for the duration of the production into a house that he was sharing with Zubi and some of the actors. Although I didn't want to be in a crowd, it would have been nice to hear his reflections on the past week and to learn from his disappointments and triumphs. Now that everyone was so busy, there were no opportunities to talk about anything other than immediate needs and concerns. I rather missed our days of planning, when everything still seemed possible and no mistakes had yet been made.

Chapter 13: The Second Week

Each day presented a new set of challenges, but I somehow had the attitude that the day's curveball had already been thrown because of the turmoil already caused by the shoot date change at this location. I was wrong.

Day 6

Before I tell you of the day's little surprise, let me give you some background. A piece of advice given to me by the entertainment law professor at SMU (the one whom I'd spoken with to try to get script clearance) was that I should choose key personnel myself so as to ensure not only their loyalty to me, but to help guarantee that I would be satisfied with them. Not following this advice more closely is a sincere regret. And no better example exists than my experience with the first makeup artist we'd hired for the film.

One of the early requests Roger made to me during pre-production was that he be allowed to select the hair and makeup artist—a friend of his. She had an adequate resume and I wanted him to have someone in whom he had confidence. However, alarm bells went off during my interview of her. She was glib, wasn't prepared to answer makeup questions based on a review of our script, and full of early demands such as what special meals she would require. She was extremely self-important and not someone I would ordinarily seriously consider. When I expressed my reticence to Roger, he assured me that I would be satisfied with her work or he would himself dismiss her. He said he really, really wanted her and promised that there was no way I'd be disappointed.

While Roger had seemed happy with her work, I saw a couple of problems and sought to discuss them with her at the end of the first week. The first issue was that she was asking the cast to do some of their own makeup. Although the cast were genial and inclined not to complain, there were some grumblings the previous week that they had been required to put on their own foundation and some basic makeup before coming to work. I told the makeup artist there were not that many actors in any given scene, so there was ample time to do all makeup and that it would be more professional if she were to do all makeup herself. I was shocked when she disagreed, saying that she only had so much time to work on actors' faces and that they had to do their part.

Another issue I brought up was to ask her to tone down the heavy black eye makeup on the lead actress and the stringy look to her hairstyle. And I was unhappy that actors some days had product on their hair and other days, not. It needed to be consistent or it could be noticeable in the film that the hair had changed from one scene to the next. Scenes are not shot in sequence usually. Thus, one has to be careful to make sure that the actors have on the same clothing and look the same physically to maintain continuity. She replied that she personally liked the heavy makeup around the eyes and that the vampy style was "in."

Her attitude and answers had made me think about firing her before the end of the first week, but I hesitated. Not only was I worried about offending Roger but was also concerned about whether firing someone would have a negative impact on overall morale. But when, over the weekend, I had heard of the incident in which she'd put black goo on an actor to simulate dried blood, and he hadn't been able to wash it off easily, I was edging close to getting rid of her. Yet I decided to give her a final chance for Roger's sake.

On the sixth day of filming, after a weekend off, everyone was present, and the set was ready for us to shoot the first scene. Cameras were ready to roll. The glitch was that some of the actors were still not made up. I had been watching the makeup artist from across the room with increasing annoyance. She was talking rather than doing makeup, and decided she needed a break when it was clear that doing so would put our schedule behind. When I quietly informed her that she needed to keep working, she replied loudly in front of cast and crew that she didn't need me telling her how or when to do her job. At this point, unpunished insubordination was more important than risking a blow to morale by firing her. I decided she had to go.

Because we were on day one of the second film week, I couldn't dismiss her immediately; I didn't want to be without an artist at all. I told Angel and Zubi to hire a replacement as soon as possible.

I was going to fire her myself. However, Angel insisted that Roger should do it. It was he who'd brought her on and her loyalties were to him, Angel argued. I said okay.

Aside from makeup problems, the filming on Day 6 went fairly well. Two examples of really good cinematography and directing stand out in my mind from this day. Both were instances when my own fears proved wrong.

The first scene was crucial to the movie. It is when the lead detective, who's figured out that the murderer is his lover, tells his partner of his discovery. I had hoped it would begin with a long shot down the hallway of the lead detective standing alone, and then move to a close up of his face to show his anguish, his despair.

The cinematographer instead had the idea of opening the scene with filming the detective through a stairwell window, across a gap, and through another window, where the detective would be looking out. Thus, there would be two panes of glass to film through, with no way to clean the windows first.

To say that I was skeptical is too mild; I even thought of interceding and vetoing the idea. I thought the lighting would be wrong and that the dirty windows would make the scene amateurish. But that little refrain I kept hearing in the back of my mind, "Let others put their creative layer on the film," held me in check. I decided not to say anything and see where the cinematographer's idea took us. I told myself to relax because if the dirty windows made the scene a mess, during editing I could cut the opening and just start with when the actors begin to talk, a part which would not be filmed through the dirty windows.

Well, I was completely wrong. Yes, the windows are smudged, and the lighting is a bit bright, but I think that the effect of both is just right. It is, artistically, one of my favorite images in the movie. I am so glad I said nothing and so happy with the cinematographer's creativity in the scene.

Also, there was a very great moment here of Roger's directing that stands out in my mind. It would have been easy for Chad to overplay or underplay his anguish and resolve at this point. Roger walked up to Chad just before the cameras were set to roll. This is exactly what he said: "Okay, you were always the cop who's seen things in black and white. But now you can see grey. Got it?" Chad nodded. It was such superb directing—simple, direct, and effective. And that's just the way Chad acted it, perfectly.

Another example of wonderful cinematography that day was when we filmed two detectives talking to one another in a stairwell. I had spoken to Roger about my enthusiasm for filming on the stairs because they are on the outside of the building and the walls are glass. It is a fabulous location. But I was worried about angles. My vision was to film the two actors only a few steps apart, so that one would not be standing too much above the other.

Instead, the cinematographer and Roger filmed the scene with one actor much higher up on the stairs, looking down at the other several stair steps away. I was again wrong, and absolutely love how it turned out. The height difference coveys a certain power to the conversation. And it showcases the architectural beauty of the building—the glass and metal with lots of appealing curves.

Aside from the snafu with the makeup artist, there was only one other thing I wish I could change about an otherwise fabulous day: the use of extras. Again, some women showed up and sat for hours waiting to be used. They could have been put to use walking around the room at the outset of the precinct meeting to do handouts, to walk down the hall, or some other job to populate the scene. But they were never used, and I felt very guilty about wasting their time.

And, speaking of extras, there was a nice surprise for me personally on Day 6. Unbeknownst to me, Angel had contacted my niece and asked her to show up to be an extra. When she walked in, I was both shocked and delighted. I am still so happy when I see her in a cop uniform serving as an extra in the movie.

Filming An Indie

Day 7

I woke up early, worried. It seemed like I went to sleep worrying and resumed immediately on waking every day. I couldn't remember my dreams but wondered if they were filled with worry too.

Today's early problem concerned a location. We were due to shoot a classroom scene on Day 10, just 3 days hence, and I still hadn't found a good venue for it. I had been working the issue steadily but couldn't reach closure. I had to focus all my attention on resolving this before I could watch today's Day-7-filming.

We had planned to use a teaching facility about 40 minutes' drive away. It had plenty of space, perfect classrooms for the scene, and great production value. But I was struggling with it. I'd jumped through hoops to get the Location Agreement signed by the headquarters of the company that owned it. Negotiations had taken weeks, many phone calls and emails, and the paperwork had gone from a 2-page document that I'd submitted to a 12-page document after they were through with it.

Now the company had just informed me that I would have to pay their staff's wages to come in and not only babysit us, but to do cleaning afterward. It came to way too much money. I decided to abandon that effort and find another place.

Previously I'd considered using the auditorium at the Mesquite Art Center, but it wasn't available on the date we needed it. Also, it was so large that I knew we wouldn't be able to get enough extras to make the room look full. Now I was considering it again.

I went back to the lady in charge of the schedule for the auditorium and sat in her office. I willed myself to be calm and genial. After telling her my story of looking everywhere I could and about my time crunch, she agreed to move the people who were going to use the auditorium for a rehearsal. I was so grateful I'd invested in being on good terms with her and for her flexibility. It solved the availability problem. Now I just needed to make sure there would be enough extras to make the scene realistic.

With the task of finding the classroom location taken care of, I hurried to the set to watch the filming of the precinct scenes, all of which were being shot at the Arts

Center. I had already missed the shooting of two scenes, and they were just starting one in which the lead detective, Coxon, learns that there have been similar crimes in Oregon to the case he is trying to solve. It upsets him because it is one more datum to indicate that the perpetrator is the woman with whom he's fallen in love.

Things went a little haywire with this scene, but before I can tell you why, I should give you background.

Coxon's character is complex, but one thing is clear throughout the script—he is a gentleman. He prides himself on being proper in appearance, behavior, and morality. He is also a lover of women. This doesn't just mean that he enjoys sex with them; he actually relishes being around them and loves to tease and flirt. One of the ways we know this is through a couple of little vignettes in the original script when he interacts with the female public relations officer of his department. He treats her with respect, as a gentleman would, but also has a playful relationship and gently teasing interactions with her.

Roger had rewritten a bit of this scene, and I had agreed to it. Specifically, he had written that Coxon would "flip her off." Those words had not resounded with me sufficiently. I hadn't envisioned that this would mean Coxon would walk away from her rudely, while giving her the finger over his shoulder. Roger also had Coxon snarl his response to the woman's question and use profanity that hadn't been in our agreed rewrite of the script. In short, in my opinion, the entire purpose of the interaction with the public relations officer had been turned on its head.

I felt that the negativity was now too far out of character for Coxon and wanted to talk to Roger, but he was coming nowhere near the Video Village where I sat. As the scene got progressively disrespectful toward the woman, a sentence that had formed a few days back was now becoming a mantra in my mind: just as there can be only one director of production, there can be only one director of post-production.

Later, I would be able to edit the profanity and bird-flipping out of the scene. However, I had to cut another clip entirely because it was too over-the-top in terms of his rudeness to the woman.

On a happier note—between takes, I noticed one of the crew wearing a tee shirt sporting the name of another movie he'd worked on. I decided to order *Revenge In Kind* tee shirts for the crew.

Day 8

We were again filming at the "precinct" and everything was going well. One of the scenes shot was when the lead character Sarah Scott talks to Gina, a rape victim, about what had happened to her. As I watched the takes from Video Village, I saw that Scott was standing, looking down to where Gina sat. I thought that no psychologist worth her salt would do that; she'd sit on-the-level and build a body-language one-to-one rapport.

At first, I hoped Sasha would say something, but when she didn't, I went to find Roger. He was in the room where the scene was being shot, which was small and filled to capacity with equipment and people, talking to the actresses. I decided to let it go and returned to the Village, thinking it could be fixed in editing. I vowed to myself to go through the upcoming scenes more thoroughly to think of such issues and try to talk to Roger about them in advance.

As I watched the filming from the Village, Scott finally sat next to Gina and something magical happened. A small beam of natural light serendipitously shone on Scott's face, encircling her scar. It was so perfect, so unplanned. I loved it and made sure to use it maximally during the editing.

Later, after filming that scene was finished, I heard Sasha telling Melissa what a fabulous acting job she'd done in that scene and that Melissa's tears almost brought her to tears too. I totally agreed. The scene is very credible and very moving. Both actresses did a superb job.

Another scene filmed on Day 8 was in Scott's office, when she talks to Detective Coxon about the murder/mutilation. As I watched, I had a similar reaction to what was unfolding as I had to the scene with Scott and Gina. My concern had to do with the relative body positions of the actors, which was not maximizing the power of Sarah Scott. Let me give you a bit of background here.

Eons ago when I took courses in theater and directing, my instructor taught me about the power of body stance—not only about a single person's, but also different people's vis-à-vis one another. A person standing full-face to the audience has most impact, full back to the audience is also powerful but less so, and profiles least powerful.

People versus one another also have more or less power based not only on their stance exposure to the audience, but also their relative height. Someone with height over another has more power, and so on. Of course, all of this is also affected by lighting, color, and texture, but the stance itself is what we were studying.

What I had learned from those directing lessons was partly why I had been concerned about Scott's standing and Gina's sitting in the filming of the scene mentioned above—I didn't think a psychologist would take a body-power position of standing and looking down on a seated patient. Now, in watching another scene being filmed, the position issue was again problematic.

In the screenplay, I had written that Scott and Coxon were on equal level, each seated with nothing between them. This is a neutral position, with no power delegated to either character by means of position. However, as it was being filmed, Coxon was standing at the corner of Scott's desk looking down at her, seated. To the audience, this denigrates the power of the seated woman subconsciously.

I mentally sent Roger the message, "Make her stand up and perch on the edge of her desk. Get her on a level with him, eye-to-eye. This woman has power, she would not just sit there with him looking down on her!" Well, of course, my mental telepathy failed, as usual.

Three other things about the day's filming stand out in my mind. One is that the playful relationship between the detectives Coxon and Kang fully blossomed, and Chester Gayao (Kang) was reaching full stride in his performance. In a hallway scene, their banter extended perfectly from what was scripted into follow-on ad-libbing as they exit the scene. This light-hearted part of the relationship stuck with their characters for the rest of shooting the movie and adds greatly to the underlying humor. Gayao's delivery had a pace and rhythm that was exceptional, so both actors were now, in my opinion, superb.

The second thing that stayed in my mind was Coxon's easy relationship with Scott. The scene where he goes in to consult with her, kissing her lightly, and then tap-tapping the desk as he departs is so revealing of the progress of the relationship. I was glad we hadn't shot this scene any earlier in the schedule—before the actors had built some rapport—or it might not have come across that way.

The third was a negative. The Laboratory brand signs are put on the door windows facing inward. On any real building, the signs would have been on the outside, facing outward. I didn't catch this at the time, or I would have talked to the production designer about it. And maybe we'd have gotten some B roll from outside the building to establish the scene.

If I had it all to do over again, I'd walk each set before filming to catch such things, but I only did this part of the time. And before you think, "Well, you are probably the only one who noticed it in the film," let me tell you that multiple people have brought it up to me, unsolicited. Today's audiences are not only savvy, but also have high expectations.

Day 9

We were now one day shy of being half of the way through filming. But it was the first day I felt we'd finally begun to sail smoothly. Everyone had got used to one another and the crew were working much more efficiently. Things seemed to have reached a comfort level.

I felt like I had not been able to watch much of the filming, so watching this day's work was a treat. Each day brought some revelation to me about the crew or cast members, and I remember that this day I especially noticed and enjoyed the actress who played Marilyn Cummins, Amanda Erickson.

I had been particularly taken by Amanda during her audition. She had the ability to convey a really wide range of emotions with her facial expressions, as well as the ability to cry when required. And, I loved her intensity. She has a stage presence that cannot be learned; she is a natural.

Roger also thought that she was very talented and suggested she might do the role of Gina well. I told him I really wanted her for Marilyn, and he agreed.

Amanda had prepared for her role very thoroughly. She sent emails outlining the wardrobe and colors for her character and had researched the role, including reading the novella in addition to the script. I therefore was already impressed, but her acting was fabulous, particularly in the scene in the precinct where she realizes that she is someone's prey and has no recourse. Her sorrow and fears are almost palpable. I'd originally feared that the plain backdrop of the scene would make it uninteresting. Instead, it allowed the acting both of Amanda and Abel Becerra (Detective Garcia, to whom she is speaking) to shine unimpeded.

In addition to the really fine acting on Day 9, I enjoyed the fact that the scenes that day showcased the creativity and finesse of Production Designer D.R. Garrett, Property Master Tyler Tipton, and Art Director Matthew Wright. The area they had to work with was originally a large room chock full of desks, workspace dividers and bookcases overflowing with papers and files. They had stripped out the clutter and created a very believable police precinct scene. It had taken a lot of thought and physical work.

One of my favorite parts of the set was the desk of Detective Sam Kang, the character from Hawai'i. The designers had read his character well. They had got a photo of the actress who played his girlfriend and framed it for his desk. Other props included a small hula doll and ukulele, reflecting his passion for Hawai'i. It may sound simple, but often what experts do is to make what is difficult seem easy and make what could be blatant look subtle.

One of the treats for me personally this day was that my cousin Fred arrived on set. He had agreed to play the small role of a detective being interviewed briefly by the lead detectives on the case. Although we didn't get much chance to talk, I was happy he was there because maybe it signaled that our rift over his demand to change the script (or else he wouldn't direct) had somewhat healed.

Jumping forward a bit, Fred's having played the role later turned out to be a huge challenge for me in editing. When I saw the scene on film, I realized that the information it contained was actually duplicative in some cases, and irrelevant in others. I hadn't seen this when I wrote the script, nor had anyone else mentioned it. But the scene clearly had no necessity for the film to make sense, and no special artistic or production value. Nevertheless, because it was my cousin, I agonized over deleting it. After our rift over his quitting the director role, I did not want anything else adversely affecting our future relationship.

One thing that helped me over the hurdle of cutting the scene during post-production was the memory of Fred's primary comment when he first read the script, "Cut it, cut it, and then cut it some more." He urged me repeatedly to use action more than dialog and to minimize talking heads. So, I knew that he was aware that any scene without fundamental value would be cut. Although I was sure he would understand why the scene had to go, I still hated omitting it. Fortunately, before I had to tell Fred that the scene was unnecessarily duplicative, he emailed to tell me that himself. I thought, what a wonderful professional he is.

At the end of Day 9, I was feeling very good physically. I went home to get some of the bureaucratic work done and took the opportunity to put together a set of emails to send out to various companies that had experience in doing movie posters. I wanted to get bids as soon as possible so that we would have some publicity materials to use within the next few months. At this point, I didn't realize that it would be best to find a company that could give me a package deal on doing a poster and a trailer. That would be another lesson learned.

Day 10

This day was to start with an outside shoot at a restaurant near my apartment, so I had been worried it might rain. But it turned out to be gorgeous and cool, with little wind. I walked to the set for our 6:30 AM start feeling great.

A studio or big production would have arranged to block off the street to traffic. But that entails not only a special paid permit, it requires hiring off-duty police to manage the area, something we just couldn't afford. Traffic, especially large delivery trucks coming to nearby restaurants, were a problem. We had to stop and restart filming a number of times because of the noise.

I told Roger that I would like to be an extra in the scene, a patron sitting at a table behind Sarah Scott. He readily agreed, but as it turned out, I almost didn't make it into my movie. The opening of the scene was shot from across the street and I am invisible behind a large planter. However, I appear briefly behind Sarah when she is speaking.

And it was good that I was sitting at the dining table as an extra. While there, waiting for the camera to roll, I learned that the extra sitting across from me had not signed a form allowing our use of him in the movie. Although that was immediately remedied, I started worrying that there might be other slip-ups with the extras. This made me more vigilant in checking on this, but I have already mentioned the snafu with tracking the extras.

After shooting the restaurant scene, I went home to write paychecks that were due the next day, finish contracts for the newly hired makeup artists, and work on getting a location for the Marilyn Cummins house, where we would need to film inside and out for three days. My hand muscles were behaving, and I didn't have to struggle like the previous week.

The company meanwhile moved filming to my niece's apartment, the place where Kang and his girlfriend June supposedly lived. Later I heard from Roger that the filming of the first scene there turned out to be such a fiasco that they ran out of time to film the second scene. The problem was that the actress playing June had not learned her lines. In take after take, she flubbed them. Not only did it cost us the time that would have been used to film the second scene, it put Roger and the crew very much on edge. I think it might have been why the afternoon's filming also had problems.

The afternoon filming, which I was able to attend, was the classroom scene in the Mesquite Arts Center auditorium. It is where Sarah Scott lectures students on the perils of date-rape drugs.

The first thing that went haywire was indecision about the location from which Sarah would speak and the camera angle. The first take has her standing on-stage, another has her sitting, another has her standing down below the stage. During editing I really wanted to use the striking shot of her back, as she stood onstage looking out at the students in the beautiful auditorium. But I couldn't use it because there'd be no way for her magically to have gotten down below the stage when she starts speaking.

And, although there are a number of takes, much of the film is unusable because there is no consistency across them. There just wasn't a clear-cut concept of how the scene would flow and the angles from which the audience would view the scene.

The second snafu was with the young actress who had the only female student speaking role. Although she'd done well in her audition, you wouldn't know she was the same person. She seemed dead-tired, always yawning, and stumbled on her lines. Her delivery was so stilted that I went to Roger and asked him to try one of the extras to see how she'd do. The alternative turned out much better, although still not very good quality. It still took a number of tries to get her nerves under control.

Much later, after my Editor Charles and I had a first assembly of the movie, we showed it to a couple of capable reviewers. One recommendation of both was to cut the classroom scene because the acting by the students was so poor and the lack of extras made the scene unrealistic. Although I agreed on both points, the content of the scene was too integral to omit it.

Weekend 2

Angel had been very worried about what location we'd find to use for the Marilyn Cummins' house scenes. I had reserved and paid for an Airbnb, but he'd convinced me that it was not a good location because it was right next to some very high-end car dealerships (with insurance implications) and near a high-traffic road (noise problems). But I was just as unhappy with the alternative he had found because it was too far away, in Forney, a town about 10 miles away, and had some location-use requirements that I was unwilling to accept. Nevertheless, it was important to have a back-up plan, so I worked on the Location Agreement for Forney over the weekend.

Something that was more fun on the weekend was working on the Facebook page for the movie and setting up the website for Pono Productions with information about the cast and crew. Also in the realm of publicity, I prepared some press releases to send out to newspapers about the filming to try to garner early interest in our production. Meanwhile, Angel set up an IMDb webpage for the film.

Another issue I felt that we needed to move forward on was music. As mentioned earlier, I had listened to a huge amount of music and made some selections of pieces

I'd like in the movie, as well as some artists. Also, I wanted to write the lyrics for the theme song, for which I would need a composer.

In August, I emailed a few composers, whose music I'd found on the Internet and liked, to ask what their prices would be to use their work. The composer I'd tentatively chosen as my favorite wanted $800 per minute of music, which was outside the realm of my budget, so I began to look at less expensive licensed music.

But I kept running into the problem of congruity. I didn't want the music to be choppy; there needed to be a thread of similarity throughout, with any dramatic differences being restricted to source music (the music that would be coming, for example, from radios or over speakers in bars and restaurants). I decided to take a closer look at composers who'd sent in emails asking to do *Revenge In Kind*'s score.

I focused on two composers whose music I liked and asked if they'd read the script and then send me a sample of what they envisioned. Also, I asked a very talented musician friend of mine (unassociated with *Revenge In Kind*) to help me evaluate the music they sent in. Even though either of the composers would have been acceptable, I was not truly happy and put off the decision repeatedly.

Zubi had a friend who is a composer in Los Angeles, Kays Al-Atrakchi. Zubi sent me some of his samples and I liked them. Then, unbeknownst to me, Zubi also shared them with Roger, who took the initiative to call Kays before I was ready for such a step.

When I heard that Roger and Zubi had interviewed a composer for *Revenge In Kind* without my permission or participation, I called Zubi and told him that, as music supervisor, I was still in the process of evaluating Kays' work and that no one else was to become engaged in the decision. I was very put off that people didn't understand the limitations of their jobs and that they weren't welcome to wander off the reservation.

I immediately got a call from Angel, who was shocked that I had "taken on the role of music supervisor." Admittedly, I had never conveyed the fact to him. But then, it had never occurred to me that he would think anyone other than me would be selecting the music.

Filming An Indie

Angel told me that he and Zubi should select a composer, and that Roger and I could participate. The composer would then be responsible for all music—composed as well as source. In other words, we would pay someone to be both the composer and music supervisor.

The struggle by others to control the post-production process was in full swing. I replied that I alone would select the composer and I very much wanted to select all source music myself. This would not only be great fun for me, but also, we couldn't afford to pay someone else to be music supervisor and find free source music, as it would be very time-consuming. We simply didn't have the funds in the budget for that. Angel agreed about the budgetary restrictions and implications.

What was occurring were the effects of my having stepped back from exercising control over the film during the production. I had purposefully stayed in the shadows because I'd wanted all the talent to have free rein for their creative input. I was willing to do that because I knew that I would be having the last say during post-production.

But now the period of post-production was getting closer and I was clearly indicating my control over the film from the end of filming onward. I was going to have the thrill of taking the "film in the can" to its final form, which was the whole point of my spending my life's savings on the project. But people just were not quite ready to release the project into my hands; it would take a little bit of wresting.

Although I actually liked Kays' music very much, I told everyone to stand down and not contact him again. I said I would interview a few more composers, then make my decision.

Meanwhile, Angel found another composer, this one in Dallas. I would have liked to have someone local, so I was excited to go to his studio and hear samples of his music. Unfortunately, his work wasn't at all what I wanted. I was comparing all candidates to Kays and none were passing muster. I decided to put off the issue of music until after the production phase.

Chapter 14: The Third Week

A busy week was ahead with filming to be done at some of our most visually rich locations. The filming would be moving a lot in terms of the time of day we would start. And, it would be the start for our two new make-up artists.

Day 11

Breakfast for the crew was at 3:45 AM at a very trendy bar called The Armoury located in the Deep Ellum section of Dallas, where old factories and warehouses have been converted to restaurants, bars, and lofts. The Armoury has an enclosed outdoor courtyard under magnificent old trees and an indoor bar with very old brick walls and a massive wooden bar along one wall. It was once a meat-packing facility, hence its name. It is an elegant set, one of my favorites in the film. Angel had found it, gotten on well with the two owners, and arranged the agreement.

The bar is the favorite haunt of the lead, Detective Coxon. In the first of two scenes filmed there, Coxon meets a prostitute and sets in the minds of the audience that this is a guy who prefers short encounters to meaningful relationships.

The second scene is one in which he demonstrates his growing dissatisfaction with such superficiality. He meets a different prostitute and tries to go beyond his usual jovial banter to engage her in substantive conversation. When he fails to do so, he leaves her and goes to meet the woman with whom he's falling in love.

The second scene was one of those that Roger had rewritten, and I had agreed to the changes. The dialog originally showed Coxon trying half-heartedly to engage in conversation with the prostitute and then apologetically abandoning her. Roger had changed it to Coxon being more aggressive in his attempts to engage her and then being brusque in his rejection of her and his departure. The new dialog was acceptable to me as long as it was not played in a way that broke his character as a gentleman.

As I watched the filming, I knew that it was being played in a way that Coxon would come across as rude rather than frustrated, nasty rather than bored. Not for the first time, I thought about confronting Roger about his not sticking with the deal we'd made. But I also debated myself. I thought again about the fact that he was being creative, adding his own layer of artistry onto the film. Then I replied to myself that he had complete freedom, per our agreement, to position actors, pace the play, and everything else about the set. The only locked in elements were dialog, story, and characters. And so, my internal debate went on and on and on.

During the filming, the Production Sound Mixer, Codi Putman, stopped the process to try to fix a problem with background noise. There was a refrigerator humming that would interfere with the clarity of dialog. But the crew couldn't get the thing to shut off. It was a built-in piece of equipment and the electricity was behind the shelving chock-full of glassware and booze bottles. We had to continue filming despite the noise.

I remember this scene as the point at which I began to work better with the wardrobe and makeup crew. I had come to realize that they didn't have the benefit of sitting in the Video Village like I did and seeing how things looked close up to the camera. I felt it more and more to be my place to be their eyes to check for things needing fixing. For example, when I saw that Coxon's tie was askew, I asked Carolina Hernandez to fix it and she did. But despite my keeping a close watch on how things looked from the Video Village, one nit got past me. Coxon's shirt collar is not lying flat against the back of his neck and looks bunched up. Probably no one notices it, but every time I see the movie, I can't help but wish that I had seen that problem in real-time.

Later in the day, we moved to the location where a scene would be filmed involving a lawyer using date-rape drug to assault a female intern interviewee whom he'd called to his home. My sister, Laurie Kidder, and her husband Bob had graciously agreed to our turning their home upside down for the afternoon to film there.

To be honest, this was one scene I was worried about in terms of acting. The actress had been a last-minute substitute for someone who'd bailed on us to take another more lucrative role. And the actor had been good in the audition, but I was afraid he wouldn't come across as slimy and evil as I was hoping. On both counts I needn't have worried.

After the filming, my sister, who watched from the sidelines, said to me, "I really want to tear the throat out of that guy." And I felt the same way. The actor, Matt Bailey (no relation to me), had successfully enraged us and his acting was so superb that I wanted to applaud after each take.

The actress, Mindy Neuendorff, was equal to the occasion. She comes across as a young professional trying hard to land a job, but with the innocence of someone new to the working world. She mixes eagerness with a growing wariness of the situation in which she finds herself. Then, her succumbing to the drug is convincingly played. It is all-in-all a really wonderful scene.

Day 12

As Day 12 started, I reflected on getting the location for day's shoot. It had started eight months before when I had made a list of the set locations we needed. At the time I thought, "No movie set in Dallas is complete without a scene in a Tex-Mex restaurant." I had searched for just the right one—an authentic hole-in-the-wall place with a lot of charm.

I had found two restaurants that would work really well. But my repeated calls to the owners and managers had gone unanswered. I even left hand-written notes to no avail. Soon, serendipity stepped in.

One day while driving down a two-lane road in a low-rent part of a Dallas suburb, I saw a row of beat-up pickup trucks parked in a narrow gravel lot in front of a low-slung building with peeling paint. The shop stood alone with no other businesses anywhere nearby. Extending out the door was a line of people, mostly tradesmen from the look of their attire. I slowed to see what the attraction was. Tortillas for lunch! I had to stop.

I found a spot to park and sat looking at the place with a critical eye. Outside is a small concrete patio with a few chairs and two tables. The walls are painted bright yellow with faded red signs in Spanish. The entry is through a tattered screen door. It looked so perfect as a set for the lunch date of the protagonist and the hero.

When the line diminished, I got out and walked in. Just inside the door is a small room around two sides of which a glass counter stretched. One side had a cash register in front of which was a line of patrons. In an alcove behind the counter was a huge blending machine into which men were dumping cornmeal all day long to ready the masa for the many hundreds of tortillas they churn out each day. It smelled wonderful, making me very hungry as I joined the line.

I was the only English-speaker and I know no Spanish, so when it was my turn, I pointed at the menu to order lingua (tongue) tacos. While everyone else was standing around waiting for their orders, the lady behind the counter came around and insistently led me to a table in a tiny dining area in the adjacent room, motioning for me to sit. Unlike the others, I was to be served. I felt very self-conscious despite how welcoming they were. While I waited for my food, I tried to envision the interior as an alternative set to the outside patio.

The dining room is only about 10 x 20 feet, with six closely spaced Formica-topped tables. It would be extremely cramped to film a scene. I wondered if it would do in a crunch if we were to have a rainy day, making outdoor filming unrealistic.

I went to wash my hands and discovered another likely problem with using this taco restaurant, El Molinito. There was only a tiny one-toilet closet which would be iffy for a 40-person film crew. If it were to break down under the heavy usage, that could be pretty bad. An alternative would be to pay for a porta-potty, but that wasn't in the budget.

When my food came, I asked if there were anyone around who spoke English. She nodded as well as shrugged. I didn't know what the answer was.

After I finished my lunch, a young lady came who said in English that her father owned the place. I asked about the possibility of using El Molinito for a film location. She looked dubious but said I could come back sometime when her father was there and talk to him about it. Then she added that he came only occasionally, unpredictably, and didn't speak any English.

Since I had doubts about using the location, I didn't push the request. It went on the back burner. I continued my search.

Some weeks later, when Angel came to town, I still had found no Tex-Mex restaurant willing to let us film there. I took him to El Molinito for lunch to get his view about using it as a location. He agreed that the outside would be perfect, but the inside would be too cramped. He said we should negotiate the Location Agreement, even if we ended up using it only as a backup. He then spoke to the staff and made an appointment to talk to the owner.

When we came back to meet with the owner, Angel said he should speak to him alone at a separate table, even though the conversation, being in Spanish, wouldn't include me anyway. That turned out to be a good tactic. Angel spoke at length with him.

At one point, Angel broke off and came to me. He said, "We are close. Would you be willing to throw in paying them to cater breakfast the day of the shoot?" That was an easy yes. I slipped him the Location Agreement, which Angel had already translated into Spanish, and the owner signed.

After all that history, here we were at El Molinito in the pre-dawn light on Day 12 of the filming. But already things were a bit out of sorts. Breakfast was supposed to be at 6:30 AM and the two women who were going to cook scrambled egg burritos for forty plus people had just shown up at 6:15 AM. They looked so tired and breakfast would be late. At least the door had been open early, and the crew was able to up the command center, make-up station, and Video Village.

As I watched the activity of setup, someone handed me a map that detailed where parking was allowed. Someone, probably Zubi, had contacted the city as well as area residents about the film activities and determined where we could park the equipment trucks and the many cars of the cast and crew. Then he had made a map and distributed it to everyone relevant. This was being done for every location where we filmed.

I was not on the recipient list for such things, as I didn't need to be. But seeing this map reminded me that there were some 40 people, all of whom had their duties and assignments. Attending to details like this was crucial to making the process efficient and smooth. Not for the last time, I marveled that Angel had assembled quite a group of experts who could make this all work.

When finally the burritos began to be served, everyone who'd been working outside crowded inside. I took one bite of my burrito and then took it outside to toss it. I was too nervous to eat. I was worrying about all manner of things, including whether the toilet would make it through the day, as I'd decided I couldn't afford a porta potty. That decision had been based on another: on Angel's good advice, we'd hired a (very expensive) licensed set medic to be on-hand for the fight scene in case anyone got hurt. I thought to myself, who would believe there is logic in the statement, "I didn't rent a toilet because I hired a medic."

Outside, I got a fresh worry as I watched rehearsal of the coming fight scene. I was told that there had been much training and several rehearsals, but it seemed to me that the "purse thief" was learning to fall correctly for the first time. Also, it was not at all clear that the thief and the protagonist, Sarah Scott, had been able to practice together. I confided my worry to the stunt choreographer, and she was apprehensive too, which only put me further into doubt. I wanted to shoot at least a few takes using the stunt choreographer, Janell Smith, as a stand in so that we would have extra footage in case there were problems with the fight. Janell thought that was a wise idea and was willing, but Roger did not want to do it, possibly because the physiques of the two women were too different.

Finally, we moved from rehearsal to filming. Angel, who watched fight scene from the Video Village with me, shook his head dejectedly. He told me that the scene might not be usable, and we might have to cut it; the action just wasn't credible. I was crestfallen. I really wanted that scene because it showed that Sarah Scott was not only mentally tough, but physically aggressive when need be. This day would be a precursor to a worry that would haunt me: that the action scenes were not believable.

But the day did have a highlight for me personally: my sister Laurie came over to be an extra. It made me feel good to have her there.

Later I was sorry that I hadn't insisted that my other sister, Andrea, also be an extra, which I think she would have loved. She died in 2017, a year after the film was shot. I cannot look at that scene in the film without thinking of her too. Forever in my mind she will be a presence that is not present.

In the afternoon, we moved from the El Molinito over to the Trinity River basin near the Margaret Hunt bridge. It is a grassy area with downtown Dallas in the background. Angel had successfully paid our film permit fee with no trouble because we did not have to depend on the film commission in any way.

The day was getting very hot, almost sweltering. I felt sorry for Chad Halbrook, our lead detective, because he was in coat and tie.

The first scene is a brief conversation between the two lead detectives. It went without problems and was in the can quickly. It was great that some extras showed up to enhance the realism of this scene. We even tapped a passing skateboarder to participate.

The remainder of the afternoon into the early evening didn't go as well. The scene consisted of a conversation between the detectives shot in a moving car. A lot of the camera work was bumpy, out-of-focus, boringly shot, or all of the above. But the sound was the worst part and most of it was unusable. I will describe the problems more in the chapter on sound.

Had I known of the difficulties associated with filming in the car, I would have written the scene to take place elsewhere. Scenes shot in cars all seem so easy on studio films, so I had unrealistic expectations.

Day 13

I was excited about the filming of the evil rapist, George Lehman (Tom Heard), stalking and then breaking into the home of Maria De La Cruz (Ada Perez). It would be a really important set of scenes, shot over two days, with two very professional, highly capable actors.

Filming An Indie

The location, an Airbnb I had rented, was perfect because it was large enough to allow for good camera work and enable crew managerial space, but also was snug enough to look like a young professional's starter home. Some of the scenes for this venue would be shot outside the home where there were large trees on a working-class-neighborhood street.

The day started with breakfast at 6:30 AM, after which the crew began setting up for filming on the tiny side porch of the house. I have a little snapshot in my mind of Gavin Chin, our Key Grip, using scissors to clip the grass under the rails on which the camera would glide. I liked it because it showed he was thinking, caring, and didn't mind doing whatever it takes to make the film right. His attitude was forever bright, cheery, and can-do.

Fairly early in the day, Angel sought me out to tell me some good news. We had been anguishing over the fact that we still didn't have a good location for filming the final scenes of the movie during the next week. Although we had a backup plan (an already rented Airbnb), we knew it wasn't even close to ideal. Angel, along with Zubi and a production assistant, had been spending enormous amounts of time on the Internet and going to scout for better options. At last, he thought he had a solution—and it was just across the street.

The house was owned by Ed and Julie. Ed approached Angel, keen to find out what we were up to with the filming going on across from his house. After a brief conversation about the film, Ed seemed open to letting us use his house for the Cummins scenes, but wanted to talk to the person in charge.

Angel asked me to go over and talk to him and try to seal the deal. I went, but it was no easy task. Ed was quite smart, but also very leery. I gave him our insurance details so that he could call my agent in LA, which he did. I also gave him the Location Agreement, which he took to an attorney who lived next door to evaluate. The attorney advised him against letting us use their place but apparently his reasons were not strong enough to deter Ed's interest.

I told Ed that our using their house would be an inconvenience because we would have to use the house all night for two nights, so I would rent them an Airbnb. They'd have to find a place for their dogs. We would be all over their house with 40 people and loads of equipment, potentially causing damage, which I promised to do my best to prevent.

After assuring Ed that we would pay a location fee, clean his house top to bottom afterward, and pay for any and all damages, he said he would try to convince his wife to do it.

Jumping ahead of Day 13 for a moment, it turned out that Julie was not too enthusiastic, so Angel and I were pretty nervous about it for two days. We really wanted the house, as it would be perfect for our needs. When Ed and Julie agreed, Ed said they were willing to take the risk because, "It is nice in life to have good stories to tell." What a wonderful way to put it!

Anyway, the outcome was that we were treated to an exceptionally great location. In return, Ed and Julie can see the film and think to themselves how much good they did by being open to helping, open to a life experience. Thanks, Ed and Julie.

Returning to Day 13, I was able to watch only an hour or so before I had to leave because it was time to write paychecks and pay bills again. And this time, there were big accounting problems.

Harald, our accountant, had emailed me a list of erroneous timesheets that Angel should not have approved. Several crew members had filed for more hours than they'd worked, some extras had put in for payment at actors' rates, and one crew member had boosted his hourly rate.

Harald was upset because he now had to recalculate paychecks and railed that this sort of nonsense should never have been signed off on. I said I'd talk with Angel later, but now I had to concentrate on going through every single timesheet and compare the rate of pay with the contracts I had for each crew member.

When I finally got the data to Harald, I had an hour or so to wait until he could send me the breakdowns for after-tax payments for checks. I spent the time being really angry about the waste of my time. I wondered if I should take over doing the timesheets from Angel, but then I would miss even more of the moviemaking than I was already missing.

There were also some other stresses that were nearing fracture. I had been agitating to get Angel to review the applicants for editor and to verify the pay range we could offer. I really wanted to get the editor on board so that he or she could attend some of the filming and start work with me, but Angel had resisted without telling me why.

Early on Day 13, Angel emailed me that he was postponing the review of editors and could not yet tell me the final budget range for paying an editor. I was ready to explode. I spent the evening of Day 13 stewing about whether Angel and I were headed toward a rift. I knew he was absolutely vital to the movie, but I was moving from being disappointed and insistent to being angry and churlish about it.

That night I drank too much wine and had a terrible bout of leg and foot cramps. Because of too much worry and too little sleep, the next day's production call at 6:00 AM seemed way too early.

Day 14

Early on Day 14, I arrived on set and looked at some takes from the previous day. I froze. I was absolutely speechless but wanted to go and yell at the people responsible for the omission that jumped out at me. What was so upsetting was that the scenes wherein the rapist enters and does his dastardly act, he doesn't wear latex gloves.

Throughout the script it is repeatedly made clear that George Lehman is a meticulous character who understands forensics. He shaves his entire body to avoid leaving DNA evidence, wears a condom, always packs latex gloves into his kit for crime, and dons gloves as he breaks in. And, in the dialog between detectives, they note that he is someone who must know a lot about leaving no fingerprints, DNA, or other traces. In other words, there is not a shred of doubt that Lehman does his heinous deeds *with latex gloves on.*

Yet, somehow, Lehman was not wearing the prescribed gloves in the scenes from Day 13. There he is, leaving fingerprints everywhere, including on door handles and the duct tape he uses to tie Maria up.

After some minutes, I reached a plateau of anger and started to calm down. Feeling very disappointed, I told myself to concentrate on the day ahead and be vigilant, to try to make sure nothing was missed today instead of thinking about yesterday. But my anger still simmered.

Around me there was hubbub of preparations to film the scene in which detectives survey the crime scene where Maria lies on the bed, murdered. The day was hot, with temperature in the mid-90s, but we couldn't turn on air conditioning because of the noise it would make. Inside the house was very uncomfortable with so many people in such a small space. It seemed to me that there was way too little oxygen in the air.

In the bedroom, the makeup artists and property master were struggling with the knife that was supposed to be stuck into Maria's chest. Despite every trick they tried, it would not stay in position; the bloody knife would just flop over. The whole thing was costing too much time. Just as I was about to suggest to them that the knife not be in her chest, but just lying beside her head, that's exactly what they decided to do. It worked out fine and we were ready to get underway.

The camera was set up in the hallway, looking in toward the bed where Maria's body lay. We did a practice run-through and then a first take.

In the scene, the detectives enter as forensic technicians are finishing up. As they stand over the body, one detective chides the other for his garish shirt. The conversation progresses, alternating between serious investigatory remarks and gentle joking among them.

I was in the kitchen, adjacent to the bedroom, listening and watching the Video Village monitor. When the first take finished, the detectives re-entered the kitchen to prepare for the next take of the same scene. (They entered the bedroom from the kitchen in the scene.)

All of a sudden Roger burst into the crowded kitchen and said, in front of cast and crew there, "Alright, we can't do it this way. We can't have the detectives being disrespectful to the body that way. They can't joke among themselves when she is lying there dead. We are taking out all the jokes." He was very upset.

Filming An Indie

In the quietest tone I could muster, I asked him what on earth was going on. He explained that one of the camera operators (a woman) was crying and was deeply disturbed by the jocular dialog in the face of the sadness of the scene. He said she was upset that the detectives were being disrespectful toward the body of a woman who'd been raped and murdered. He said he felt she was correct; we can't have detectives being disrespectful to the dead woman.

I said softly, trying to make the discussion just between us, that the script had been read by him and everyone else. The dialog had not been changed, so they should all have been on board with it. I said that whoever was having a meltdown was probably doing so in response to unrelated stress and that she needed to be told to behave more professionally. I ended by noting that he had agreed to direct the script as written. I said we were not going to change the story or the scene just because someone was getting emotional over it.

Roger didn't back down. He said defiantly, "I just can't shoot it that way. I won't do it."

I was trying really hard to keep myself calm. I wanted to go in and yell at whoever had lost a grip on their emotions. And I wanted to scream at Roger, "Do your damned job!" But I checked my own reactions and looked wordlessly at Chad Halbrook, our lead actor, asking with my eyes for help. Chad immediately read me.

Chad stepped in front of Roger and said that joking is how people handle bad situations. It is totally normal, he said, for cops to joke among themselves in the face of a murder scene because it is a coping mechanism. He ended by firmly saying, "We have to film it the way it is written."

Roger replied that we could change the script a bit to make it less offensive. Both Chad and I took turns explaining that it wasn't offensive, that the cops made no remarks about the body, the girl, or her death. They merely chided one another with meaningless prattle.

Chad told Roger we needed to get back to the filming and to do it the way it was written. "Let's not waste any more time," he said. Chad then turned away from Roger and to everyone said, "Let's go."

Roger followed and we returned to filming. It was remarkable to me that no one in the cast or crew seemed affected by the to-do. I was very grateful for that. I was also thankful for Chad's intervention and later told him so, to which he replied that it was the right thing to do.

After that incident, I vowed that if I ever did another movie, I would have the cast and crew sign a statement that they'd read and understood the script, and that they would in no way object to its being filmed as written.

Day 15

It was the last day of our third week of filming. It was a late-start day, with production call at 2:00 PM. But my day had to start early because it was another payday and I had to hand out checks before filming was to start.

Once again, there were problems with erroneous timesheets to sort out. But sometimes when you've been through a problem before, encountering it again doesn't seem so dire the second time around. Or maybe the timesheet issues didn't seem so problematic in comparison to the morning's other challenges.

One was that an actor, whose role in the film had already been shot and he had already returned to Los Angeles, was on a tirade. He called me, screaming mad because taxes had been deducted from his pay.

I tried to explain that we were required by law and code to hire him as an employee rather than as a contractor. Employees have taxes deducted; contractors don't. He demanded that his status be changed to contractor and that we not withhold taxes. No matter how I tried to explain it, he would not be mollified.

You can be reasonable in the face of shouting; you can be calm in the face of rage and expletives; you can hold firm despite demands and threats. But doing so takes an emotional toll, or at least it did on me.

After I'd finished dealing with that actor, I had to do some contracts for three substitute hires for crew who needed to take a day off. My mind was so distracted from the emotion of the ordeal that I kept making mistakes and had to re-do them a couple of times.

When I finished the business matters, I turned to the script. Today we were to shoot a few scenes, including one on which Roger and I had not reached agreement. When he first presented the changes, he wanted to make to the script, he hadn't included today's addition of a scene in which Sarah Scott, the police psychologist, breaks into the rapist George Lehman's home. In Roger's changes, Sarah creeps up to the lump on the bed, throws back the covers, and sees a note that says, "I found you Sarah!". Then a fight ensues, she gains the upper hand, then runs away.

It seemed hokey to have the note. It seemed unrealistic to have her break in, presumably to kill him, and then depart without killing him when she got the upper hand. But most of all, it seemed totally out-of-character for her not to have planned better. She would have had her Taser, as she did in all other cases, and would definitely not have been foolish enough to get close enough to the bed that he could have sprung on her. To me, the whole scene stuck out like a sore thumb as being an add-on, one that added no useful meaning, and diminished the competence of Sarah Scott's character.

I went to the set to hand out the checks and stayed for only a couple of hours before it was time to go and do Pono's insulin. Although I intended to return, I ultimately decided not to for two reasons. First, the space on set was very limited and even one more body would make the situation more cramped. Second, I just didn't want my negative energy about what was transpiring to be present. Maybe, I thought, the scene would be done so very well that later I'd look at it with fresh eyes and see great value. If I didn't, then it would be cut.

Some of the most superb footage of the film was shot that night in scenes that were in the original script. The creepy images of George Lehman shaving his body, watching and getting off on videos of his past crimes, talking insanely to the dismembered marionettes in his room—all these were perfectly played and filmed beautifully. But the add-on break-in scene by Sarah Scott turned out to be even more of a disaster than I'd feared. Not only did it not fit the story line well, the action of the fight scene was a flop. Scene cut.

Weekend 3

Early in the morning on the first day of our third weekend, which was a Friday, I got a call from the owner of the Airbnb where we'd filmed on Day 14. She was apoplectic, saying we had destroyed her house, making it unrentable. She listed a host of problems: nail holes in the walls, a strip of white on the hardwood floor where tape had ripped off the finish, "blood" stains on the comforter and sheets, and excessive trash in the bins.

After letting her scream at me for a few minutes, I asked if I could meet her at the house to assess the problems. She said no, that she was sending her husband and son and that I was to meet them there. Frankly, I was a tad fearful and didn't want to go alone to meet two angry guys. I called Angel to get him to join me. I also tucked a couple of hundred dollars in my pocket and quickly drafted an agreement for full, complete, and final payment for damages.

When we got there, the son and husband were indeed very angry and showed us the damage. Other than the strip of finish missing from the floor, I didn't think any of the problems were either very significant or irreparable. We offered to fill the tiny nail holes, take the linen to get it cleaned, and to haul away all trash even though it was inside the trash bins belonging to the house. Then I offered $200 as reparations for the floor, which to me looked like normal wear and tear. They calmed down, took the money, and signed the agreement I had drafted stating that it was sufficient payment for all damages.

As soon as I got home, I thought I had better cover myself with Airbnb. I emailed to tell them that I had caused some limited damage, had paid a cash settlement, and had a receipt to that effect.

It was good that I took this little step because later in the day I got an email cc in which the house owners had written to Airbnb that I should be charged for a host of repairs. The house owners had greatly expanded their list of damages that we'd supposedly caused. Oddly, they added a complaint that we had repaired a broken toilet, which was true. And they made no mention of the cash payment or their agreement to that being payment in full. Thankfully, Airbnb investigated their claims and found in my favor.

Filming An Indie

I told Harald about the fiasco and he noted that crews often get lax toward the end of production as they increasingly tire. He suggested we start emphasizing clean up and care in our daily morning crew briefings. Angel and Zubi did this and I think it helped. Also, Angel personally began to oversee the treatment of locations, to include such things as covering floors and using non-pull tape. (Going to Home Depot to obtain said tape and covering added to my own tasks.)

For the remainder of the weekend, I worked with Harald on payroll taxes. I also spent some time thinking about post-production more seriously. I decided to explore placing the movie on streaming platforms once it was finished in case no distributor wanted it. I found online information on companies that could load the finished film onto digital streaming platforms like Amazon and iTunes and emailed four to ask for telephone interviews to understand their services and costs better.

Also, I had another telephone interview with Charles Willis, a prospective editor in which I was interested, even though Angel was negative about him. Angel sent me an email suggesting that Charles couldn't meet the requirements for a 4K film product, so I asked him to interview to Charles to make sure of what he could or could not do.

Angel was holding out for either of two editors in Austin who'd done several studio features. I called both of them and found that they would charge almost five times what Angel had in the budget for editing. But I didn't feel like arguing more about this because we'd been over it so many times already.

We weren't going to begin filming on Sunday, Day 16, until 2:30 PM, so I vowed that I was going to get as much sleep as I could because the next day's shoot was to be in my apartment and it would go into the wee hours of the morning. But that wasn't to be. In the night, I repeatedly awoke gasping for air after I'd quit breathing. I stayed asleep for no more than 30 minutes a stretch all night. In the morning, I was very tired and scared that the muscles in my chest were getting much weaker much faster.

Just as you can remember being in pain, but you cannot (thankfully) neurologically re-create pain, you cannot retrospectively feel the dissonance and anguish of depression. But I can recall that I was terribly depressed that night of October 8, 2016. Roger had distanced himself from me, removing any semblance of the collaboration that had been present at the outset. I could see clearly that chunks of the film were going to be unusable and I worried that they'd be crucial bits. And troubles with Angel on the editorship and managerial bumps were troubling me increasingly. But these woes were dwarfed by the nagging reality that my mind sought so hard to ignore—impending death. There was absolutely no question that my fasciculations and cramps had increased in frequency and intensity in the past month, and that my muscles were much weaker. Breathing often seemed no longer an act without thought.

I got up fairly early and composed an email to my attorney in LA, asking her to prepare a document that would assure that all rights to Pono Productions and the film would go to my heirs upon my death. I also went over all of my beneficiary designations for my accounts. I now believed I wouldn't make it to the end of 2016.

Late in the day, Angel called and said that we had a dog shit problem. Ed and Julie had two large dogs and they pooped in the side yard, where cast and crew would need to walk during the filming in the next few days. Angel said he would arrange for Dogey-Doo, a poop removal company to come, but I needed to get written permission from Ed to have it done.

I laughed, thinking he was kidding. When he persisted, I asked, "Who would care if we removed their dogs' crap for them?"

He was right when he replied that we were contracting for someone else to come do work at their house and it would be bad if something went amiss and we had no permission. I knew Angel was right and thought again how lucky I was to have him on the film, thinking these things through and taking care of problems.

I duly got hold of Ed to get written permission to remove his dogs' poop. Ed thought it was a pretty funny request.

Chapter 15: The Fourth and Last Week

The weekend had been so busy that I was mentally not quite ready for the fourth week to start, but here it was. And the first day of filming was to be in my apartment.

Day 16

My condominium had rules against any commercial activity taking place after hours as well as against heavy equipment being transported through the lobby. Because we would film from 3:00 PM to 3:00 AM, I needed to get the Board of Directors to approve exceptions to both rules. I also had to make sure that my neighbors were informed and didn't mind the filming.

In addition to these mundane and time-consuming hurdles, plans had to be made for the crew to move everything quickly into the building in less than 30 minutes to minimize disruption and to maintain silence in the hallways. All of this had been done and I felt we were on track. What I hadn't counted on was a couple of drunk residents almost derailing us.

It was about 10:30 PM when one of the residents began to get in the faces of the crew who were working quietly outside my apartment door. He was very angry, claiming that we were breaking the rules and that everyone in the hallway, including equipment, be removed. I explained to him that we had Board approval and that we were being very quiet so as to disturb no one. Rather than accepting this, he went to call the Director of the Board to complain. He apparently claimed that our crew, even if everyone were quiet, could be a danger to the building. He said that they could go unaccompanied to another floor and perhaps break into one of the condos.

What he demanded, and got, was a couple of employees of the building being called in (on overtime, because it was late at night) to monitor us. One was put on my apartment's floor outside the elevator and another outside the basement elevator. Both employees got chairs and promptly began to doze. But even if they hadn't fallen asleep, what purpose could they serve? It was a ridiculous waste of money done simply to make management look like it was doing something constructive in response to a resident's complaint. If the "elevator minders" had mollified everyone, I guess it would have been okay. But more trouble was afoot.

As soon as the minders had taken up keeping elevator vigil, another resident took inspiration from the first. This one was even more inebriated. He loudly proclaimed we were in violation of the rules and began to video the crew and scene preparations with his phone. I tried to talk him down to no avail. He became increasingly agitated and began to hold his phone about an inch from my nose as the spittle from his yammering mouth hit my face. I slapped the phone way and he began to howl that I had attacked him. Well, this was now beyond me. I called the police. As soon as he understood that I was really talking to the police, he scurried away.

In my experience, most people are uncomfortable talking to uniformed police. It takes a certain confidence and a dose of ego to see them either as equals or lesser. Therefore, I figured that I would be the one to interact with the police, especially since I was involved in confronting the resident. However, there was another person whose self-confidence was akin to my own and who stepped in to take over—Zubi Mohammad, our production manager.

Zubi explained calmly that it would be better if I backed off now and let him handle things. I gratefully agreed, as I was feeling the aftereffects of adrenaline laced with accumulated weariness.

When the police came, Zubi masterfully handled the situation and the police tried, but ultimately failed, to get the resident to delete the videos he'd taken. But the main mission was accomplished: the drunk didn't bother us again. The rest of the night went smoothly.

Now to relate the really important events of Day 16, let me turn to the only bedroom scene of the film. You may recall that the cinematographer, Terra Gutmann-Gonzalez, had asked me how I imagined the scene and I had described to her a shot akin to John Lennon and Yoko Ono in bed, as seen from above. The lovers, after sex, are talking. When he asks about the scar on her face, she abruptly leaves the bed.

I think the shot from above turned out to be spectacular and the rest of the scene worked well too. But, interestingly, this scene later presented one of the greatest editing challenges to me and my editor, Charles Willis. I will jump ahead here to tell you about Day 16 from the editing point-of-view.

The problem was that both actors got out of bed with their underwear on. I had assumed that Roger and Terra could somehow finesse the filming to make it credible that the two had just made love. For example, maybe they'd have the sheets positioned in a way that obscured the actors' briefs, have them wear nude-colored underwear so that the colorist would have a prayer of a chance of fixing it, or at least have a shot of buttocks. But that wasn't the case.

Charles and I tried dozens of ways to cut the scene using every take we had, but it just wouldn't work. Her underpants were bright Kelly green, making it well beyond our budget to convert them to flesh. His were thigh-length grey shorts seen not only from the back, but front-on, so editing that wasn't in the cards either.

Ultimately, we had to cut all views of her exit from bed and have her lines heard only from off-stage. With him, we had one and only one useable take of his getting out of bed seen only from the waist up. All of the rest show him throwing back the sheet, revealing that he'd apparently just had sex with his underwear on. We then spliced in another take, one in which the actor had popped the waistband on his underpants. This enabled us to craft the sequence so that it looked like he'd just pulled the underwear on. I thought we were pretty lucky to put it together in a way that looks fairly credible, although it was a shame to have had to edit the actress out of the scene.

Day 17

This day marked the beginning of the end of filming. All remaining scenes over the next four days were to be shot at the house of Marilyn Cummins, the character who is stalked by the rapist/murderer George Lehman. Day 17's scenes were all outdoors, with the first one being where he sits in his truck staring at her while she gardens.

Just as a side note, this scene was originally one in which she was jogging and he followed her slowly, videoing her. Moving from the original concept to one which was easier to film was interesting to me as a screenwriter. I learned to think more about the practicalities and finances associated with different ways of portraying an action. Static gardening is far easier to film than two subjects moving in tandem. Although it would have been interesting visually to have motion as a tool to express fear—for example having her speed up jogging as she notices him following her—it also worked well to have a good actress, which we had, build the tension visually in her face, eyes, and hand motions.

Two things stick out in my mind about this stalking scene. The first has to do with the value of a scripty, a person who is tracking how the filming of each take of an individual scene matches up with the script. The Lehman character was filmed from the passenger side of his truck, focusing on the back of him looking out the driver's window at Marilyn as she gardened. He was videoing her with his phone.

When we began the second take of that scene, actor Tom Heard changed the hand with which he held the phone. Our scripty told him to change back to the other hand and to keep it that way for all takes.

He said, "But I was holding it with this hand in the first take."

"No, you absolutely were not. Change hands."

And she was right. I hadn't noticed that. But had she not interceded, it would have been a problem in editing if we had wanted to used parts of more than one take because the audience would have noticed the inconsistency of which hand was holding the phone.

The other thing that I remember quite clearly was when Marilyn turns her head to notice Lehman, sitting in his parked truck, staring at her. When she notices him, Roger directed him to wave at Marilyn and she was instructed to wave in return. I was mentally pacing and growling in displeasure at this. I decided to act.

Just then there was a "bathroom break" called and Amanda Erickson, who played Marilyn, walked around to the side of the house. I intercepted her and asked, "Do you feel that your character would wave to a stalker? Would any woman? Is this realistic?"

She replied that she did not think it realistic at all. I told her that she needed to let the director know if something is out-of-character. She agreed and made sure we had takes without the wave.

Day 18

This day began with crew call at 7:00 PM and I was unable to attend the filming at all. I had spent the entire day working on film issues and was again having severe foot cramps. I was too exhausted to stay up all night. Later when looking at the film shot, I was sorry to have missed watching some superb acting, directing, and cinematography that night. But watching the filming was not on my mind much; I was getting extremely anxious and angry over the delay in choosing an editor.

Choosing an editor ideally should be made prior to filming so that they can be involved from the start of production. As it turned out, I didn't choose anyone until after production was completed even though I had wanted to and tried. The central problem was that Angel and I were in dispute over two issues: money and the degree of control I'd have over the editing process.

Angel held out hope that somehow, we would have enough money left over after production to afford an editor experienced in editing feature films produced by studios. The nearest of those that we knew about was in Austin and when I had called them, I learned that they cost more than five times the money we had budgeted for the editor. I could not get Angel to accept that there absolutely would be no more money and that we would have to change our expectations.

The other issue was that Angel wanted to turn over the film to someone with totally fresh eyes and who would not be under my instruction. My goal was to edit the film to the vision of it that I had in my head. This was a basic disagreement that was never bridged.

That night I had a meltdown about the editorship—a conniption fit with tears and gnashing of teeth. By phone, admittedly emotionally weakened by too much wine, I told Angel I could no longer bear the indecision and I planned to move forward with choosing an editor myself and that I had decided upon Charles Willis. Charles was keen to fulfill my vision of the film, was local so that he could meet with me, and was willing to work with our budget. If Charles could handle the editing software professionally, that was all I needed to know. I was alternately demanding, wheedling, and angry throughout the phone call.

Ultimately, Angel agreed that he and Zubi would interview Charles in a conference call to make sure that he was up to the job technically. If he were, that would be followed by an in-person interview.

Over the next couple of days, Angel talked to Charles and gave an "okay, but with reservations" verdict. He suggested that we interview some more candidates. I said no. Too much time had been wasted and I was satisfied that Charles would be capable of working with me to bring the film together. I spoke no more with Angel about the editorship. I sent Charles a contract to sign and took over the process myself.

I did not involve Roger in the selection of editor. He had asked a few times if he could edit the film himself, so I feared he might not be supportive of any editor I selected. But I still planned to involve him in the editing process. I felt that without the cast and crew around, he would not feel his authority undermined if we worked collaboratively. But I decided not to mention Charles to Roger before I had Charles fully on board.

Jumping ahead for a moment, Charles turned out to be a wonderful editor. He was genial to work with, he wanted to help me achieve the film I sought as best possible, and he was able to work well with the editing technology.

Day 19

Crew call was at 7:00 PM and I was on set. I didn't want to miss at least the first part of filming this night because it was the fight scene that Roger, Janell, and I had worked on so hard in my apartment in the pre-production period. Both Janell and I were apprehensive after the problems with the fight scene at the taco shop, and I also was worried that Roger would try to reintroduce the dialog that he'd agreed to leave out. If this scene didn't look real, it could be devastating to the credibility of the Sarah Scott character and the movie overall.

While there is no question that a big studio production could have done the fight scene much better, the action was pretty good and none of the problems I'd fretted about came to pass.

There were little glitches, of course, and one of them was of particular interest to me as the screenwriter. In the screenplay, I had not made the sequence of actions crystal clear, so they ended up being logically inconsistent. Here is what happened.

A detective goes down the stairs, where the murderer is hiding in a closet. The detective starts to open the closet door but is immediately distracted by a noise beyond. He turns to investigate that noise, thus allowing the murderer to come out behind him and cut his throat.

But how did that distracting noise conveniently occur? There is no logical explanation for it in the film, so the audience either has to ignore it, or be left confused.

In retrospect, I should have written clearly that the detective does not approach the closet door, but rather is checking the place out when the murderer slowly opens the closet door behind him and then kills him. The audience would have been in on the suspense, seeing the murderer sneak up on the detective. The audience would have been edgy, willing the detective to turn around, and horrified when he does not. It was yet another "woulda-coulda-shoulda" moment for me.

The filming that night was going so smoothly that I felt really relaxed. Then my feet cramps set in. I couldn't stand comfortably, but if I took my weight off my feet by sitting, they would curl with a pain that I was afraid would be visible on my face. I decided to leave. I was glad I did because I missed knowing about a very worrisome end to the night.

We had a total of three trucks rented for the movie, the smallest of which was a U-Haul that we used for a couple of things, including the digital imaging technician's very expensive computers and drives. And, more important from my perspective, the cargo included the priceless film shot that night. That truck, with the others, was parked every night at the MPD where it would be safe. But this night, it wouldn't start. As with the incident on the first night when the lighting equipment truck wouldn't start, Angel stayed with it. The toll on him was pretty severe. He was already perpetually exhausted from the long days, but to have to spend his night hours protecting the truck was too much.

The next day, U-Haul tried to argue that the truck would not start due to lack of fuel, which simply wasn't the case. It took a lot of arguing to get them to bring a replacement. We had a lot of other troubles with U-Haul, including when we tried to settle the bill. I wish that there had been a reasonable competitor to them available to us.

Day 20

The last day of filming had arrived. I had spent the day writing checks for the cast, crew, caterer, and a few others, as well as working on trying to tie up some mundane loose ends with insurance and the attorney. I had put in a full day of work before the evening crew call at 7:00 PM, but I wanted to see at least the outset of the shoot. I gave Pono her insulin, fed her on time, and set off to watch the last day. I took along with me the tee shirts I had ordered for the crew to hand out.

There was a lull in activity when I arrived, so I handed out the black tees—with *Revenge In Kind* on the front and *Crew* on the back—to the crew members. Every recipient thanked me. Only one person do I recall saying anything more than that. He said, "Oh, wow, these are actually good quality. Maybe they'll last a while." It made me happy that someone noticed that I had sprung for the best.

This evening's shoot included the final scene in which Sarah Scott dies in Chris Coxon's arms. I had been ambivalent about Scott's dying, not really willing to see such a bold, audacious character end. Others working on the film had expressed unhappiness about her death too. I had even gotten an email from a crew member asking if I couldn't rewrite it to have it be ambiguous about whether she actually died. We had all grown so fond of Sarah Scott!

Early that evening, I was talking during a break with Chad, who played Chris Coxon. I asked him whether he thought there should be room for doubt about whether Scott's wounds were mortal. He said that there was not a shred of doubt that Scott died; it couldn't be otherwise. I knew that too, but it was nice to hear from the character that had fallen in love with Scott that he accepted her death as a necessity of the story.

Scott's death, to me, was a highlight of the film in addition to the climax. The reason was the way in which it was acted. Chad Halbrook did an exceptional job portraying the grief over and horror of her death. Anyone who has experienced witnessing the death of a loved one can totally identify. Also, Sasha Higgins did a wonderful job of portraying how death really is. Too often I see actors who "die" in a film maintain an energy level in their face, eyes, and body posture that is commensurate with the fully alive. That just isn't the way it is in reality. Death slowly drains away a person's energy, their vitality. The dying person slumps, has difficulty breathing and speaking, and their eyes lose light. Sasha played it like it really is.

Another memory of that night was when I was leaving the set around 1:00 or 2:00 AM. Some crew were out at the street curb behind the equipment truck spinning a bicycle wheel on a tripod. Wanting to find out what they were up to, I went over to say hello. They asked me to guess what they were doing, but I couldn't, so they demonstrated.

They put the spinning wheel together with some red and blue lights. They were preparing the lights for the emergency vehicles that would flash outside the window of the bedroom at the end of the movie. I thought it was absolutely brilliant and asked how they came up with the idea. They said they'd learned it in film school. The idea sure beat having to pay for renting a cop-car light bar.

Day 21

Filming was over and now the house we had used the past four days needed to be made spotless, per my promise to Ed and Julie. Two PAs were on hand to help me. Today, I would be the executive who plays janitor.

I entered the now-quiet house. Angel stood in the kitchen staring at his laptop screen, his face haggard and body weary. He had been up and working way too many hours. He said, "Zubi is totally worn down. He almost passed out. I had him lay down on the couch downstairs and he is zonked. Do you think you could take him home to get some sleep? I have to get the IT trailer over to the Art Center so that Laurel can finish working the film and get it onto all three hard drives."

I said I would and went to get Zubi. I could hardly awaken him. It was almost scary; he was so unsteady and woozy with sleep. I got him into the front passenger seat and the seatbelt on, whereupon he fell asleep again. I got him safely to the house where he and some others on the film were staying, then returned to begin the house cleaning.

Our use of the house really showed. Forty people had made use of the three bathrooms throughout more than 12 hours each workday. The floors were still covered with protective board and tape. Cups, food, and trash were everywhere.

I had the heavy lifting done by the two assistants. They pulled up all the floor protection and carried it out. When cleared, I told one to vacuum the floors and the other to pick up trash while I dusted, scrubbed the kitchen, and cleaned.

I was carrying a load of trash out when I saw the gaffer getting out of a car containing some of the other crew at the front curb. They had been to breakfast and were now having a beer. The gaffer got in the equipment truck to drive it away. As he left the curb, I wanted to scream a warning. Every other day he had been careful, but just now he plowed forward and the top of the truck hit a huge thick tree branch with such force that it fell. It was so big and heavy that it later took two men to drag it out of the street.

The branch tore a gaping hole in the upper corner of the truck. That one little moment ended up costing me $1500 in repairs. Our insurance deductible was that much, so it was all out of my pocket. As I rued the moment, I tried to tell myself that it was a great good fortune that no other accidents or mishaps had occurred during my dear film's production.

I returned to cleaning and as I was sanitizing and brushing the toilets, I thought about what a range of jobs I'd done: writing, producing, location scouting, so many things, and now cleaning toilets.

Filming An Indie

I finally sent the assistants home and finished up myself. After another two hours, I sat down on the couch to wait for the owner to come and inspect the house. After he had looked it over and approved, I handed him the location use check and thanked him for his and his wife's bravery in letting a film company use their home. He said that it was his pleasure because doing such unusual things are what make life interesting. I totally agreed.

I then headed over to the Arts Center to check on the status of the film. I was expecting to see what I had seen the day before: a massive pile of props (some of which I intended to keep for my own use, like a potted plant, or a souvenir, like one of the marionettes); tons of food, condiments, and sodas; blankets and sheets; wardrobe clothing. I had thought it would take me a day to sort it all and decide what to donate to charity.

But none of it was there! All that remained were a few cases of soda. I asked where it all had gone, and Angel just shrugged. My guess is that he had told whoever showed up to take what they wanted and that was alright with me. I wouldn't have any mementos, but I didn't plan to be around long to enjoy them anyway.

Laurel, our DIT, looked tired but happy. She carefully put a 4 TB hard drive in its box and handed it to me with a proud smile. Angel said, "K.C., at last you have your film." I got goosebumps as I accepted the box from Laurel. I hugged her.

Angel, Laurel, and a couple of others were packing their things up to leave and go get much needed sleep. I hurried to get out of there because I didn't want to be the last one there. I was already feeling lonely and a sense of anxiety about the next steps. Watching them depart would exacerbate that.

I learned that the cast and crew would have a party at an outdoor restaurant that night. I do not know whether I was not invited because I had not thrown the party for them, but they probably knew I didn't have the money to do that. Angel said that I was not invited because I was the executive and would put a damper on things. In any case, I did not really want to go because I am deaf without hearing aids and still hard-of-hearing with them, particularly in noisy environments. I just wish I had had a chance to thank them at the end and tell them goodbye. The were a great group and had worked very hard.

Getting An ALS Test

By the end of filming, I was having huge difficulty sleeping. It was not just the cramps that usually awakened me in the wee hours, I was also increasingly suffering from apnea. I would wake up gasping for air, knowing that I had quit breathing. When I finally would fall asleep again, the whole process would repeat. I suspected that the muscle problems that were causing the cramps and fasciculations in my feet and legs had now moved to my chest, but I was not sure.

Although I didn't have much hope of a solution, I wondered if I should now be on a breathing machine of some sort. In early November, I went to a different doctor, a neurologist, who decided to give a closer look at whether I really had ALS. He administered an electromyogram, which measures the signals that run between nerves and muscles and the electrical activity inside the muscles. It involves sticking needles in you and a mild zapping, which is pretty uncomfortable. He also did a nerve conduction study to see the rate at which the nerves respond to an electrical impulse.

His diagnosis was that the results were not consistent with ALS, but he was not willing to hazard a guess as to what else might be the problem. He suggested more invasive tests to try to find the cause. My father had had those tests and they had been not only painful, but inconclusive, so I was unwilling to try those yet.

With regard to the breathing problem he suggested a sleep test to see whether my apnea was sufficiently bad to warrant a continuous positive airway pressure machine (CPAP).

I was absolutely thrilled that he concluded that I probably did not have ALS. But what could be the problem? Was it likely fatal? Was there something that could be done? I now had hope and was reinvigorated to find out what was going on with my muscles and nerves. But first I would start with the sleep test, as the doctor suggested, to see whether my breathing could be helped.

The results of the sleep test showed that my apnea index was 11, meaning that in 7 hours of sleep, I had just over 70 events in which I would stop breathing, causing a sleep disturbance or an awakening. My oxygen level dropped to 76% at its lowest point (88% is usually considered the baseline below which it should not fall). So, indeed, it was time for a CPAP.

The CPAP made a huge difference in that I slept a lot better, but the cramps and fasciculations were unmitigated. Since the neurologist agreed there was something very wrong, but didn't know what, I decided to do some more intensive research on the Internet myself before any further tests or going to yet another doctor. I had done such research months before, but this time I was going to try to read scientific and medical journals which are harder to understand because of their vocabulary and jargon.

K. C. Bailey

Chapter 16: A Few More Days

I expected to be happier with the filming ended. I guess it is somewhat like postpartum depression. All the excitement, activity, and planning are over. The product is there, freshly born, and you cannot go back in time.

I went home and sat down in the silence of my apartment and thought, "What now?" I had lived every moment for the past nine months to get to this single point. I knew it was time to shift gears. As everyone knows, a film is made three times: in its writing, its filming, and in its editing. It was the beginning of the last stage. But before the editing could begin, there would be an interim period in which Angel and I tidied up some loose ends.

B Roll and The Drone

After production, Angel moved back in with me for a couple of weeks. One of the first things he wanted to discuss, to his great credit, was that we either didn't have enough B roll or that the B roll we had was unlikely to be appropriate. (B roll is film that is not the actual takes of the movie, but is visual material used to transition between or add to scenes.)

The drone shots we had were not particularly relevant to the film. They were of things like railroad tracks, traffic, and bridges—none of which related to any of the scenes nor helped establish time transition. Also, we didn't have much B roll from the actual production film locations either.

Filming An Indie

Angel said it would be best if we could hire Sparky Sorenson and his drone for one more day. We discussed our priorities: more daytime shots of the exterior of the police building and of the Mesquite Arts Center (aka our "college"); the boathouse on the lake; and nighttime overhead shots of traffic.

I fretted about the exterior shots. In just the few days since production had ended, the weather had turned quite cold and the trees had started to turn. We would not be able to get shots outside that meshed seasonally with the rest of the film. This is why it is so important to get B roll at the same time as you film production.

Angel said that we'd just have to hurry up, do our best, and see if we could get anything usable. So, I hired Sparky and his drone, and we set a schedule that would begin in the morning and go well into the night, another 12-hour day.

We headed for the Arts Center first and to get some exterior shots of the "college." That took more time than anticipated, partly because Angel said that if I would like to be in the movie, it would be good to have some B roll of people walking across the college courtyard. I wanted to be in the movie, so I eagerly agreed. [In editing, I did not use this footage because I didn't think that it fit well, to my regret.]

Because of the extra time filming at the college, we were in a bit of a hurry when we got to the police department. Our objective—to get some overhead shots of the beautiful steel and glass building to help establish for the audience each of the scenes that were shot there—needed to be done while the light was still good.

I already had permission from Mesquite and MPD to shoot the exterior of the police building, although I hadn't specified to them that any shots would be taken from a drone. Since I didn't think the drone would come close to the building, I decided not to bother anyone inside with a notice that we'd be doing drone shots that day.

In the MPD parking lot, we discussed with Sparky that we'd like to have a shot going from one end of the curved building to the other, filming in an arc, at about the level of the top of the building looking down and from afar. We didn't want to get any directly overhead shots or to get close to the building at all. So, Sparky programmed the drone to go from one end of the building (point A), to the middle (point B), to the other end of the building (point C), then back again to achieve a scanning, rounded shot of the whole structure.

It was the very first shot of the police building from the drone that day....and the last. Sparky programmed A, B, C, A instead of A, B, C, B, A. That meant that the drone would cut across the building rather than following the same arc on the return. And, because the drone was not too high up, it clipped the edge of the roof, and crashed onto it.

The part of the police department roof where the drone crashed was flat. But the rest of the building was actually higher than the flat portion and had office windows overlooking the flat expanse of the roof. As you can imagine, there was a flurry of response as police officials inside witnessed a drone crashing onto their roof.

Those who know what true dread feels like will understand when I say that my adrenaline kicked in and my heart raced as I realized what happened. It was a mixture of concern about the poor drone, and a bit of "oh no, we won't get the shots now", but mostly a fear of what the police would say and do. Would there be a fine? Would they give us the drone back? What on earth will I say to them? How will I explain our actions and my lack of getting additional permission?

I told Sparky we had to go in right away and try to claim the drone. Angel said he didn't want to be any part of it all and walked away. So, into the building I went, Sparky trailing behind, and talked to the Sergeant on duty. "Yes," he said gruffly, "we already know about the drone. Stand right there. Someone will be down shortly."

I thought to myself how quickly he'd been notified, as it had been only a matter of a couple of minutes since the disaster. And the scowl that accompanied that "stand right there" made me very apprehensive.

Sparky and I were then put into a small room to wait, where I began to rehearse what I would say to try to get the drone back. We stewed for about 20 minutes before a plain-clothes officer came. He said, "Well, you certainly caused some excitement."

I explained how the mishap occurred and he told us that they were not yet sure how to retrieve the drone because the roof was sealed, and they hadn't yet found anyone who had the ability to access it. He told us to wait while they tried to locate someone. It was a very long, suspenseful wait.

At last we were taken to go onto the roof. We had to climb a very narrow set of stairs that were unlit, dirty, and dark. The step risers were so high that I struggled, going up on all fours in absence of a handrail. At the top of the stairs was a quite heavy hatch that had to be pushed upward. The very strong cop with us groaned as he shoved and heaved.

While the policeman minding us waited, Sparky and I went across the roof to retrieve the crippled drone. It was sad to see Sparky examine it so lovingly and with such sorrow. But I was very, very grateful that they allowed us to have it back.

It took several days before Sparky could get drone replacement parts, and meantime the trees turned even further. Although I wished we could get more shots of the police department, I decided not to try. I told Sparky to call us when the drone was ready, and we would see if there was anything else that we could usefully shoot.

Angel Does Time-Lapse Photography

While we were waiting for Sparky to get the drone operating again, Angel explained why we really needed more day-to-night B roll. In some cases, a daytime scene is followed by a night-time scene and going between the two would be confusing unless there were some visual clue to help the audience make the leap. Or there might be a lapse in time, and you need to convey that passage.

Angel explained that almost all of the B roll for *Revenge In Kind* shot during production was either day or night, which is useable only for transitions of scenes that are day-day, or night-night. What we need instead was day *and* night shots taken from the exact same spot, or perhaps some single shots showing evening turning to dark. He added that the majority of the B roll taken during production was shots of traffic, so it was of limited use.

Angel had a brilliant idea. He proposed getting a time-lapse controller for my SLR camera and getting a sequence of shots from my balcony of the Dallas skyline from afternoon until after nightfall. We purchased the controller and Angel set up the camera. The result was wonderful; it not only helped emphasize the location being Dallas, but it was also useful to mark a time transition.

Angel also had the idea to do the same sort of sequence over White Rock Lake, another landmark in Dallas where we'd shot two scenes. We got up before the sun and headed out. It was frigid. Angel set up the camera and then we waited, stamping our feet and rubbing our hands together in a futile attempt to stay warm. Finally, we got the sunrise sequence and headed home. I wished later that we had done the same thing in a few other locations.

Night Drone Shooting

At last Sparky had the drone parts and we were ready to get a bit more B roll. Angel and I talked about what would be most useful and decided that the change in the tree colors definitely precluded that would be the most ideal. Instead, Angel suggest that we do some night filming.

We decided that it would be good to have a shot of the attorney's house (my sister's home) as well as some aerial shots of cars moving on roads. The latter would be particularly useful in transitioning to a scene wherein two detectives arrive at a victim's home at night to check it out. The scene immediately before this one is when the detectives are talking in the precinct about going to the home and, unfortunately, it is shot in daylight. We wanted to have something to break the timeline from that activity at the precinct to when they arrive at the home.

When we went to my sister's house to film the outside of "the attorney's house," the exterior lights were off. Angel asked me to get my sister to turn on the lights, so I rang the doorbell. No answer, but I knew she very likely was home. I telephoned, but again no answer. Suddenly her cat Delilah showed up and started meowing. I went out to the curb and texted my sister that her cat was at the door and was hungry. That made my sister come out to pick up Delilah, and then we got her to turn on the lights. We got our shot of B roll of her house.

The remainder of the filming that night was a little nerve-wracking. I was afraid the drone would crash into tree branches because it was so dark. But Sparky was comfortable that he could keep the drone high enough and move along with it to keep it safe.

Angel drove my car. We were communicating by phone. I would watch for when there would be no other vehicles coming and tell him to start driving. Sparky would then track the car, filming from the drone. We did this over and over, trying to get the timing right vis-a-vis other traffic on the road. It was really cold outside, and I was happy when we finally got the film we needed. I was also happy when it was over because we were landing the drone in people's front yards and I kept worrying that someone would object, or worse, hurt the drone before we could get to it.

Had I appreciated the importance of B roll more, I would have assured that a number of shots of scenes without actors were filmed. I already mentioned that it would have been wonderful to have footage of the two professional kilns at the artist's studio. Similarly, it would have been helpful to have film of the length of the bar in the bar scene (where we had extras that are not in the movie as a result of not shooting that bar), several close ups of the marionettes in the villain's apartment, footage of the outsides of buildings that were used for interior filming, and so on.

My advice to anyone contemplating making a film is that they go through the script in advance and mark where it is likely to require B roll and to specify what type of shots and lighting would be ideal. This is certainly what I'd do if I could do it all over again. This may seem like a totally obvious recommendation, and I am sure studio productions do it routinely, but it is a fact that none of the professionals working on the film thought to do it.

K. C. Bailey

Chapter 17: The Outset of Editing

Sometimes I read a really good book and get excited about seeing the movie version. Then, the movie turns out to so different from the book that I am disappointed. When that happens, it is usually because the dialog is too much at variance from the book, the characters are redefined, or the plot is changed—or all of the above. This phenomenon is perhaps why I like legitimate theater so much. A play is a defined, accepted plot and dialog, even though it can be adapted. The production of the play can vary greatly in terms of the sets, costumes, and even the timeframe in which the play is set. Shakespeare's *King Lear*, directed by Richard Eyre in 2018, is an example. It is set in the 21st century but maintains the play pretty much as written in 1605.

When I set out to make a movie from the screenplay *Revenge In Kind*, I approached it much as I would to make a stage production of a play in the sense that I wanted to maintain the story line, the characters as developed in the plot, and the dialog. There were a huge number of unknown variables that would be determined by others, including costumes, props, sets, lighting, acting, camera artwork, and direction. To me, direction was critical, as it would determine how actors were positioned, as well as their movements, expressions, and line delivery.

When I began the process of supervising editing, I had my original objective in mind. I wanted to assure that the final product incorporated as much of the agreed-upon screenplay as feasible and to maximize the scenes and takes that kept the characters true.

One Director Of Post-Production

After filming ended, I called Roger and told him I had hired Charles Willis to be editor and gave him Charles' email address. I told him that I would have the last say in artistic decision-making, but that I wanted the three of us to work together. I said that we would get started the following week.

I then took the hard drive to Charles so that he could start looking at the scenes and get a feel for what he would be working with. The next day, I got a call from Charles, who told me that he had just received emails from Roger about how to begin the editing process and giving instructions. He said Roger wanted to open the first scene with shots of tabloids with headlines about crime in Dallas. Charles asked me if I knew about that and if I approved. I said no to both. I was bothered by the fact that Roger had not cc'd me on his emails or made any move to coordinate or collaborate.

Charles then gave me a familiar admonition with a twist. He said, "There can be only one director of post-production. I need to know whether it is going to be Roger or you. I can't spend my time trying to figure out who to listen to or resolving differences of opinion. I think Roger has a very different vision of the film than you and we will end up arguing all the time if someone is not in charge. So, tell me now, is it you or is it Roger?"

I replied, "I will direct post-production. I know how I want this film to turn out and I need you to help me attain the reality from the vision in my head."

Charles said, "Good to know. Let's get going. How do you want to start?"

Our plan of action was to start through the film in sequence with the scenes as arranged in the screenplay. We knew we could later reorder the sequence, but it would be a useful starting point. My role at the outset was to go through all of the takes of any given scene and to select those that I thought best and provide them to Charles. He would give me his opinion on the quality of the shots, any ideas he had about positioning, or other thoughts. Then I would go through each scene again, making notes about the time frames and their juxtaposition so that Charles would know who and what is being shown to the viewer at any given point in the dialog or action. Using these notes, Charles would lace together the scene and give it to me for refinement, together with any comments he had.

We had 20 days' worth of film from production. On each day, we had shot between 55 and 65 takes, each of which averaged between 2-3 minutes in duration. That meant we had about 50 hours of film to go through in addition to several hours of B roll. Charles and I first watched everything we had, then began to select the best takes and string them together to see what we thought might be the best progression for the scenes.

Omitting the Word *Fuck*

One of the first things I did was to set some basic guidelines. An example was whether or not I would include profanity or rude gestures.

There are some words that are so overworked that they have lost their gravity and grandeur. Think of *awesome* as in "Man, your shoes are awesome". *Awe* is "a feeling of reverential respect mixed with fear or wonder." Now really, are shoes (save Dorothy's in *The Wizard of Oz*) ever really awesome?

Or think of the word *literally*. Someone told me, "My headache was so bad that my brain was literally exploding." I couldn't help wishing I'd seen that.

Fuck is similarly overworked. These days it is primarily used to emphasize, often with a tinge of anger or disrespect. And common speech is so sprinkled with it that it has lost much of its cachet of obscenity.

Although I am far from being a prude, I decided early in drafting *Revenge In Kind* that I didn't want lazy dialog littered with the word *fuck* or other profanity. But could I have dialog that would be realistic without expletives? Answering that took me more time than you'd imagine. First, I analyzed the characters to decide if their personalities and mode of speech would be more realistic and truer if they said *fuck* a lot. I decided that indeed there was one character who would be more authentic if he did: a character named Brown.

In particular, there is a scene in a bar in which Brown gets really angry. I absolutely know that if he were to verbalize, he would not only say *fuck*, he would call someone an asshole, etc. I thought about this a while and decided that I could actually make his anger even more powerful than his voice and those words would convey; I could have him smash a beer bottle and threaten with it.

Writing the screenplay with interesting, realistic dialog—but without the use of obscenities—became a fun challenge. But I promised myself that if I ever felt that authenticity would be enhanced with such usage, I would insert it.

But the screenplay is, of course, not the final determinant of what the dialog is in the film. Although Roger had agreed to the locked script and not to change the dialog, that did not obviate *fucks* creeping into the actors' ad-libbing. Although they were fairly good about not doing that, there were two instances that indeed appear in the film, and one that was edited out.

The one I omitted successfully was spoken by a woman being interviewed by the police. In a couple of the takes, the actress had added the word *fucking* into the sentence, "I wasn't going to have a fucking conversation with him." But she was just as convincing in the takes without it. In fact, many viewers can probably imagine the word *fucking* right before *conversation* just from the way she delivers the word *conversation*. Since her character is a young, well-educated professional who's supposed to elicit sympathy from the audience, I felt we could do without the expletive.

But there are two that stayed in the film. Actually, the first ad lib of *fuck* is not totally complete. An actor who plays a villain is set upon by a vigilante. He looks in surprise and says, "What the f....!" Even though he enunciated the F sound without the "..uck", I thought about whether it should be edited out. I decided not to. However, the English closed captions as well as the subtitles in foreign languages went ahead and finished the word. I told the subtitles company to change it to just "f...".

The second ad lib of *fuck* got by me because of my poor hearing. An actor is departing a room angrily and says, "Don't say another fucking word." He is off-stage and the sound could easily have been edited to omit it had I known it was there. It is faint and many will not notice it unless they are watching closed captions or subtitles. Still, when I found out about it, I was pretty fucking disappointed.

The Actor Couldn't Smoke

When I was developing the character George Lehman, a creepy but very smart rapist and murderer, I kept seeing him in my mind as a smoker. I didn't have a good reason for this other than I see smoking as an addiction and he had an addictive personality, one that suffered a compulsion to abuse women. Making him a smoker was, to me, an added layer of disgusting behavior to his personality.

It never occurred to me that it would be hard or impossible for a really exceptional actor to not be able to fake smoking. But that is what happened. One of the finest performances of the movies is by actor Tom Heard, who plays Lehman. Tom was able to convey a wide range of emotions and make his character very, very frightening. (His performance was called out as exceptional by one of the two reviews the film received. More on that below.) Despite his talent and incredible portrayal of Lehman, Tom could not convincingly smoke. Even though the cigarette is fake, Tom seemed to dislike the action of smoking and did not pull off making it integral to Lehman's behavior.

I was not present during the filming of the scene in which Lehman is smoking as he lurks behind a tree, stalking his victim. But in the takes I saw that Tom puts the cigarette quickly to his mouth, sucks a tad, and immediately blows out the "smoke". No scenes of the lurking were shot without this unrealistic smoking, so I ended up cutting it very short to try to hide the odd way he handled the cigarette. So, if you plan to make a movie with a smoker, make sure the actor is on board with the action and is able to pull it off.

In editing this scene, I had a writer's retrospective moment. I was thinking of ways I might have lengthened the time that the film would reasonably focus on Lehman lurking behind the tree in order to better register his evil and satisfied expression. One way would have been for me to include his crushing out the cigarette on the tree bark, then carefully pocketing the stub. This would also emphasize his dedication to leaving no traces.

Boom Operator

When the debate raged some years ago about whether women should be allowed in combat roles in the US military, I was a strong defender of allowing it. This was not because I thought some women could attain the physical strength and endurance that many men can. Rather, it was because I saw the nature of war changing, with technology playing a larger role and the needs for physical strength being in many cases replaced by mental and psychological capabilities. Nevertheless, I always acknowledged that there were physical roles that most women would never be able to perform as well as many men. As in the case of the military, I think there is at least one role in the film business best filled with a man— boom operator.

When I began to review the takes of *Revenge In Kind*, I noticed that there was a disturbing frequency of the boom bobbing into the film frame. Over and over I had to tell Charles to edit the boom out of the take. Sometimes I even had to choose a less desirable take simply because he was unable to edit the boom out without pushing in and clipping too much of the frame.

The problem was that the female boom operator had to stand still for long stretches of time with her arms extended over her head. In her hands she held a length of metal tube with a microphone at the end. That boom must have gone from feeling like it weighed a few pounds at the outset of filming to a ton as the day wore on. Her arms couldn't take it and as she shifted around trying to keep the boom aloft, it would bob in and out of the scene.

In one case, there were no takes in which the boom, and even the operator herself, did not appear. That scene, in which the woman being stalked hurries to her door, enters, and looks fearfully out at her stalker, was too good and necessary to eliminate. Charles could not press in on the frame enough to eliminate the problem, so I said to leave it. I was hoping to solve the problem during coloring the film after editing.

Indeed, our colorist would work hard with the problem, darkening the background to try to fix it. Even though he worked wonders, I still see faint outline of the boom and operator when I watch the movie, even if others may not.

Moving Props

A really irritating issue that happened with us, but that would likely never occur with a studio production today, is what I will call the phenomenon of the moving prop. This is when a noticeable item is moved in between the takes of a given scene. Editing is greatly restricted when this occurs. Let me give you but two examples.

One scene takes place in the police meeting room. In it, the police captain introduces psychologist Sarah Scott, who has just been added to the force. Charles and I wanted to use a few of the shots of her from different takes so that we could go back and forth between her and what was happening elsewhere in the room. This would have allowed us to use more of her different facial expressions.

The problem was that an extra was positioned very visibly behind her holding a coffee cup. In each take, he had been instructed not to move until everyone applauded, in order to avoid his being a distraction. However, he did not consistently hold his cup in the same hand or at the same height. That meant we had to choose between using only "right-handed takes" or "left-handed ones." This reduced the options of showing her by about half.

A similar issue happened a few times elsewhere, but it did not affect editing to the extent that the second example did—which was in the scene where the attorney drugs and rapes a female interviewee. In this scene, her glass unaccountably moves between takes. Again, this restricted out being able to use parts of the various takes that otherwise we would have.

First Assembly

Angel had told me that the editing process should take only about four weeks. That may be accurate for others who are experienced, but I wasn't. Although I was spending between eight and ten hours a day every day in front of my computer, I could not rapidly choose what to omit and how to interlace what I wanted to keep. I could not even order the scenes with finality. In particular, I could not decide how to open the movie because the timeline of the screenplay no longer seemed right and I was going to have to re-order the sequences.

Several times early on I thought of Angel's admonition that I could not do this job and that Charles was not the right choice for editor. Then I would remind myself of the most important point of all—this is my joy ride, and I paid for it. This helped me accept my slower pace of editing.

The first effort, finished in early November, was way too long. I wanted to use pieces of too many of the takes, which would make the film well over two hours long when

I was aiming for 90 minutes. But I thought it was a first assembly, so showed it to Angel and Roger.

Angel lambasted it, saying that there was no way this could be called a first assembly. He said I was taking on a role for which I was neither trained nor experienced and again argued that for the sake of the film I should not undertake "supervised editing" and should spend the money (that I didn't have) to get a new editor to whom I should turn over the film. He was so angry that, I later learned, he called my cousin Fred to complain. Fred then emailed me, saying that I should fire my editor and hire a new one. He added that Angel could do a better job at editing than was being done and that Angel had already sent him samples of how he himself would do the editing.

Even though Angel was very unhappy with my first effort, he did try to help me. We set up a time for a phone call for him to give me specific feedback. I wasn't sure why we had to make an appointment but found out soon enough. The phone call lasted three hours and fifteen minutes. The basic take-aways from the call, aside from technical aspects such as angle of shot or how long to remain on a subject, were that the pace needed to be quickened throughout and he wanted to delete many of the scenes that I liked.

One of the useful takeaways from the phone conversation, which I don't think Angel intended or would have liked, is that I became more comfortable with my interpretation of the film and preferences for little clips. Let me give an example.

Angel noted that the murdering rapist goes to the closet in which his victim is hiding and pauses. He gently rubs his forefinger across the doorknob before grabbing it and jerking the door open. Angel said to cut that part; the audience knows the door has a doorknob, that the guy is going to open the door, and thus the pause is a waste of time. Angel said the film needs to keep moving quickly with much faster pace.

My reason for keeping the clip with the finger on the knob was to insert both art and emotion. The guy is relishing what he is about to do, and his pause gives him a second to savor what is to come. The miniscule pause also gives the audience a little longer to fear the inevitable.

Roger's response to the first assembly was kinder in tone than Angel's, much less detailed, but also gave a bottom line that the editing sucked. He emailed me that he had more editing awards than he had room to display and that he would do a great job with the film. Of course, he was right on that count. He would have known what he was doing better than I and would have done well. But he missed the points that we did not share the same vision, it was my film, and I was having fun—or, at least, I was beginning to.

Several days later, on November 23, I unexpectedly received a forwarded email from Angel from the original sender, Luke Asa Guidici, who is a director and screenwriter. Unbeknownst to me, Angel had given him the first assembly and he had gone through it, labeling which transitions were abrupt, which scenes didn't seem to go anywhere, glitches in timing, and a host of problems identified according to their timeline in the assembly. It was very useful for a couple of reasons. It was written, so I could consult it without having to rely on memory or scribbled notes. Also, I found the format clear and concise, so I started using the it to give my ideas and feedback to Charles. An example of the format is in a sample of my notes to Charles below.

Also at the end of November, a reviewer whom I did not know personally but who had been recommended to me, called to tell me his impressions. He had some criticisms such as "the actress looks at the floor to see the marker where she is supposed to stand" in the scene where the pizza arrives. I used his comments to filter out a few clips. The one thing he opined that was in synch with everyone else's remarks was that the action scenes were not good. When I said we would re-edit them, he said, don't bother, the raw materials just aren't there.

Filming An Indie

Notes To Charles

Scene Subject	Time	Question or Suggestion
Sarah's office	whole	46/2 better for when she calls him back, he's more quizzical looking.
	46:45:21	Use 46B/1 where he looks away.
	46:57:21	Remove "I get those women."
	48:24:01	Omit line "So you trust me…" and his turnaround in response.
	48:32:00	Keep "Hey, hey!" but omit "I'm not done with you."
	50:33:08	Stay on him till after "second time ask out" line. Too choppy to switch to her during.
Brown crime	52:18:17	Can clip out the guy on the right dusting the top of the door? Why on earth look for fingerprints there?
Kang's apt.		Love what you did with this!
Bar/PW#2		She is expensive escort, so would not be smart-mouthed or sassy. Edit to change whole tone.
	56:15:11	Cut from here to 56:21:16, so it opens with him looking bored. then go to a shot of her (not talking) to show that he's with an escort.
Lehman's house	1:00:45:13	Remove all dialog. Point is he likes to review his crimes, not that he's plotting next rape.
Taco Shop	1:02:53:15	Keep on wide scene until after she asks "Does it work?" Then switch to close in of him in 60C giving answer about flies up there. (Try 60C/2 the part at the very end of the take.) Maybe keep the piece you have starting at 1:03:01:14. Then back to 60C.
	1:04:08:23	Coxon shouldn't holster his gun until AFTER she says, "No, let him go…"
Hospital	1:17:21:22	Use 81B/2 because it shows the attorney in the room as well as him staring down the nurse.
Boathouse	1:20:24:03	The only two takes that she gets the lines correctly are 83B/4 and 83B/6. Change to one of those.
Scott's Apt	1:25:02:12	Insert face view from 1:25:42:11 here; omit all between 1:25:05:11 to 1:25:16:02. Add audio of her saying the words.
Precinct hall	1:26:36:01	Add in the ending from this scene that is in the take 83/3 starting at 1:24
Lehman's house	1:27:40:00	Camera too unsteady. Try to get this one rock solid if can. No grunting. Music will carry.

Chapter 18: More Editing Issues

Some scenes we had filmed were unusable for various reasons. But cutting them might have significant ramifications such as omitting necessary information for the audience. This meant that Charles and I would have to examine all the remainder of the scenes for actions or information that might not make sense due to omitting the unusable scene. Then those scenes would have to be cut or edited accordingly.

Cutting some of the scenes also was sad for me because a couple of them were important either because they were filmed at really great locations, or because they forced us to omit scenes that would have added greatly to character development. Two examples of scenes I did not want to cut, but did, are described below.

Cutting the Murder of Brown

Bruce Brown is a rapist and murderer who has gotten away with his crimes repeatedly. Woman In Black, one of his prior assault victims, is out for revenge. She steals into his apartment, tazes him, ties him up, and gives him a chance to beg for forgiveness. But he is combative and unrepentant. Convinced that he is no longer worthy of life, she kills him and cuts off his penis and stuffs it in his mouth.

The scene is essential to the movie in three respects. First, it is character introduction. This scene is the initial appearance of Woman In Black, who will appear elsewhere in the film. Without this early introduction to the audience, subsequent appearances of the Woman will be confusing.

Filming An Indie

Second, the scene develops the character of the Woman In Black. The actions and dialog make clear that she is a forceful personality, one who has her own moral standards that are both fair and tough. The scene is to reveal her rage and power. She is willing to take risks and to mete out punishment, including execution.

Third, the murder of Brown is a crime that police will be investigating for the remainder of the story. Without showing Brown's death, the rest of the movie does not make sense.

I was not able to be present during the filming the night this scene was shot. But I knew it hadn't gone well when, the next day, I asked the lead actress, Sasha Higgins (who was normally very circumspect and non-critical), how it had gone. She shook her head ruefully and said, "When we finished, I asked myself what on earth we had just done. I am not sure it is good at all."

With dread, I later watched the takes. Sure enough, the scenes were nothing like originally written and were just awful. Instead of the Woman In Black angrily standing over her tied up victim demanding that he confess to his crimes and repent, she is demurely seated across the room where she speaks to him in a low-level monotone. The powerful female had been reduced to a meek and ineffectual wimp. The entire dialog, intended to reveal why she was seeking revenge, was altered and unusable. To top it all off, her wardrobe looked ridiculous and eye make-up like a raccoon's. Nothing about the scene was credible.

I wanted to reshoot the scene and direct it myself. But there were too many obstacles. The actor who had played Brown was from LA and had already returned home; the Airbnb where we had filmed was no longer available; I did not want to insult Roger; and, to re-film would mess up the entire schedule. I was fervently hoping it could be somehow salvaged.

Although I did not talk to Roger about the fiasco, I received an email from him a day or two later. He lamented that the filming had gone horribly that night and he felt the film was unusable. He suggested that I be prepared to use none of it, or to cut it to the bare essentials.

In editing, I ended up cutting the scene down to only a few moments—just enough to make it clear that Woman In Black kills Brown. But I think we may have lost more of the film that night than just the scene we had to cut. In retrospect, I have wondered if the direction of that scene set the tone for how Sasha Higgins would play her character. Would she have played the woman more forcefully throughout the remainder of the film had she played her character as tough in that scene?

Cutting the Gym Scenes

One of my favorite film locations—the Mesquite Police Department gym—had an excellent layout, varied machines, and great ambiance with a modernistic blue aura to the lighting. I had invested a lot of time and effort into the negotiations for it because I thought it was so special.

The location was where two important scenes occurred. The first—let's call it encounter 1—is when the lead detective and the police psychologist have their first interaction. This is a stage-setter and was designed to visibly portray the strength of character of the police psychologist; she is exercising, demonstrating skill and power. The detective is observing, clearly impressed.

Encounter 2 in the gym is when they were more advanced in their relationship. It is where the audience learns that their relationship has moved beyond the professional into a personal one.

Encounter 1 had been rewritten at Roger's behest and, although I agreed to it, I was dubious. In the rewriting, the lead detective was irritable toward the psychologist, even disdainful. I was bothered by this because it seemed out-of-character for him to be rude and I couldn't see the point of having antipathy injected when it was to be reversed only a few scenes later. So, to be honest, I was unhappy with the content, but was ready to let it happen and see if it worked. I thought that if the dialog turned out not to work, we could always use the exercise portion to show her character.

During the crew's set-up for Encounter 1, when there was little for the actors to do, the lead actor was exercising and doing pull-ups. As previously noted, I asked Roger to stop him to save his energy, but he said for me not to worry, that he wouldn't get tired or hurt. I knew better but didn't want to make an issue and disagree in front of personnel.

Filming An Indie

I didn't stay to watch the filming that day, so I only learned of the results during editing. They were too poor to use for multiple reasons. The takes where Chad, the lead actor is bench pressing were progressively ridiculous. With each take, his effort was more and more strained—like he was trying to work on weights that were way beyond his physical capacity. He had become overly tired.

Even though I loved the location, the scene was unacceptable on three counts: the hostility of the lead detective was out-of-character, inexplicable, and served only to confuse rather than elucidate; the iron pumping in the most usable takes looked silly; and, unexpectedly and unfortunately, no amount of training and practice before filming made the police psychologist look like an athletic, trained expert in karate.

Encounter 2, shot at the same location, was when the psychologist and detective are working out together, talking face to face. I didn't know until I started the editing that Chad had injured his wrist during exercise before or during filming Encounter 1. Now it was wrapped in a mess of white tape around the wrist and hand. It was glaring, distracting, and begged the question of what was wrong with him.

The bandage was not only white, it was bulky. To remove it with special effects would be too much of a challenge and would cost more than our entire effects & coloring budget.

I considered having the entire scene be a conversation with his voice in the background, but only showing her. But that raised a different problem. She was working on a machine in which her arms were bent in an L, with her hands beside her head, pressing forward, supposedly against resistant weights. But there was no weight on the machine. So, it looked totally effortless (and was), like she was playing, not exercising. Again, it looked silly.

There are important lessons I should have already known. Don't allow actors to exercise on-set and let them use only minimal physical effort prior to actual filming so as to guarantee fresh energy. Don't allow bandages or other distracting elements to costumes. Also, if there is supposed to be physical resistance, make sure it looks real. And the best way to do that is to have it be real.

Because of the irreparable flaws in both scenes, one was entirely cut and the other was pared to the bone. It was a waste of a beautiful location.

Cinematographer Craftwork

Usually problems are more memorable than non-problems, which is of course why troublesome scenes stick out in my memory. But there are also some memories of when I thought there might be a problem, but it turned out just fine. One example of such was when the cinematographer had envisioned things differently—and better—than I had.

In the script, the vigilante was supposed to walk toward her sleeping victim and stop near him. She would pick up a photograph on the table and gaze at its subjects—him, his wife, and children. She would slowly shake her head in disgust and replace the photo. The point, of course, was to show how even rapists can have families and appear to have "normal lives."

In my initial review of the takes, there was no close-up of the photograph. Without that, the audience would have no clue as to the purpose of the vigilante picking up the photo. The message that the rapist had a seemingly ordinary family life could not be conveyed without that close-up.

I was sad about the lack of film coverage of the photograph, but without it, there was no point in having the vigilante pause for it. So, for the sake of pace and want of message, I cut the entire "photo gazing" part of the scene. I felt unhappy that the "regular guy" aspect of the rapist wouldn't be made.

Later, I was going through takes in preparation for editing another related scene—one in which the rapist greeting his intended victim at his door. There it was, the close up of the photo of the rapist and his family!

The cinematographer had filmed the photograph in the foreground, with the rapist greeting his intended victim in the background. What an artful way of conveying my "regular family guy" notion! My original objective for having the photograph had been achieved in an entirely different way, and one which was more subtle than the original plan. Rather than hitting the audience squarely with the message, it is delivered obliquely. This was a lovely instance of having another artist on the film come up with a creative idea to do something that I liked much better than my own preconceived notion.

Extras Problems

A problem that showed up in the editing process had nothing to do with the actual filming and everything to do with management—accounting for the extras. You need to know who each extra is and to have their permission to use them in the film. Otherwise, you might be sued.

The right way to have handled extras was to obtain their contact information, a signed release, and a photo of each so that we'd subsequently know who each person was. I wasn't careful enough to give this job to someone able and to make sure that they did it. I just trusted that they knew their job because they said they did.

As I worked on the editing, I realized what a mess I had on my hands. It was very time-consuming and onerous for me to identify all extras and make sure that there was a signed release for every one of them that appeared in the movie. The job was much more arduous than it should have been because the person in charge of extras had not done her job well.

For example, there is a scene where some "students" are sitting in an auditorium. There was no written record anywhere of the names of the extras in that scene. Looking at the film clips I wanted to use, I had no idea of who was in the film or whether we had proper, signed releases for them.

Fortunately, I had kept all the emails I had sent to people who might serve as extras, and those emails were my only hope of identifying the individuals. I spent many hours combing through them getting the names of people who, based on their time availability to be in the film, could possibly be in that student scene.

I then took a still shot from the film that contained all the students in the room. I digitally circled each face and put a letter next to it. Then I emailed the photo to every possible extra that could have been in the scene, asking if they were in it and, if so, to tell me which letter identified them. Fortunately, all of the people in the photo replied as to where they were in the photo. I then cross-compared names with the release forms to make sure that we had legal authority to include each one in the film. What an ordeal!

If I hadn't been able to identify them, the scene would have either been eliminated or cut very differently, adversely affecting the quality. The process shouldn't have been necessary if someone had just been properly tasked and had done her job. Yet it was my fault, as a producer and the one in charge, not to have made sure that it was done right.

Editing Out Adolescent Behavior

One of the interesting elements of editing Revenge In Kind was the realization of very different interpretations between Roger and me about the purpose of a few of the scenes. Specifically, he was willing at points to interject actions which to my mind were adolescent, but to him (or so I imagine) added movement and a new layer of purpose to the scene. I felt some of these changes resulted in altering the mood if not the purpose of the scene. In some cases, it also impacted on the nature of a character. Let me give you one example.

There is a scene of a meeting that takes place in the police squad room. In it, one of the three detectives working on a case briefs the others on what is known about the perpetrator, which is very little. Then he turns it over to the chief, who proceeds to introduce the protagonist, Police Psychologist Sarah Scott. What is supposed to be accomplished in this very quick scene is threefold: summarizing what the police know about the crime, letting the audience know Scott is a PhD and what her role is in the police department, and showing the lead detective's the interest in and approval of both her looks and credentials.

Roger changed the scene markedly. He directed one of the two detectives sitting in the squad room to throw a paper wad at the detective who is giving the briefing. That detective, in turn, throws it back. The action exchange, if left in, would dominate the entire scene and swamp the information imparted verbally and by facial expressions.

Roger also directed the lead detective, who is supposed to be enamored of Sarah Scott and with whom he is shortly to fall in love, to smirk at her introduction and pointedly not congratulate her when other fellow officers do so—a total change from the original objective.

The new direction turned the scene on its head. The first problem is that the detectives are made to look juvenile and, by doing their antics in the presence of the chief while he is talking, disrespectful. I could see no useful purpose to this alteration, so Charles and I worked harder than we otherwise would have had to in editing the scene to omit the wad throwing. The second part of the change—making the lead detective look disparaging—was something I could do little about.

As I was editing this scene, and a couple of others with similar issues, I wondered if a female director would have refrained from introducing adolescent behavior and attitudes. I will never know, of course, but I surmise that a woman would have seen such actions as detracting from not only the information content of the scene, but also the interplay between the characters that was the original objective.

Omitting the Name Mesquite

When we got the permit to film in the City of Mesquite, I had received verbal agreement that if we filmed somewhere and the name of the city appeared, there would be no problem, especially since we were going to list the city at the end of the credit roll. However, my attorney subsequently advised that the permission for the city name to appear in the film be in writing.

I phoned my contact Carol, who was our main helper and problem-solver from the city. She was away at a conference but returned my call the following week. As we were making friendly conversation at the outset of the call, she told me that the conference she had attended was on expanding tourism and conventions. She had been particularly interested in a session on cities hosting film projects. She commented that we were fortunate to have got the filming permit when we did because we might not have been successful if we were filing now. I asked why.

Carol was immediately reticent and tried to redirect the conversation. I said, "Let me just ask one question before we change topic. Did you talk to the Texas Film Commission people? Were they there?" She replied, "Yes." So, TFC had struck again.

We turned to the reason I had called, which was to get written permission to use the name of the city. I explained that we had fabulous shots of the exterior of the glass and steel city building that we wanted to use, but that the city name was embedded in the front. Per my attorney's instruction, I wanted to get permission in writing.

Carol said she didn't want to give it to me herself and possibly get in trouble, so told me I needed to talk to the newly hired city attorney. She gave me the attorney's number, adding that she was not sanguine about my chances. I asked why, was the attorney at the conference too? Yes, she was.

It took days for me to reach the attorney. She kept not returning my calls. When I at last spoke with her, she was icy and close to nasty. She said that her view was that we absolutely could not use the city name in any of the scenes of the film. I told her that I had previously obtained verbal permission and asked if she would consider consulting the city officials about whether our permit could be amended to include using the city name. She said she was not willing to ask anyone anything and that, in any event, it was her decision that would be determinant, not theirs.

We blurred out the city's name where we could. In some cases, we simply did not use shots that we wanted because they did not look good after trying to blur.

When we were ready to finalize the credit roll for the end of the film, I wondered whether there would be any hassles resulting from our stating where the film was made and thanking the City of Mesquite. After all, everyone had been wonderful to us, save the irritable attorney. I wrote an email to Carol and asked her to provide in writing that we could use the city's name in the credit roll. She got permission and emailed it back to me.

Chapter 19: A Poster, A Trailer, And Music

Angel said that he knew how to arrange for a poster to be done by a company in Los Angeles, so I took this off of my to-do list early on. It made sense to me that the poster would be based on the finished film, so I was happy to wait. With 20/20 hindsight, I should not have.

Poster art should be considered early in filmmaking so that you can plan to take optimal still photographs of scenes as they are being filmed or actors in their makeup and costume. Because I did not do this, I had to rely on stills extracted from the film. (Alternatively, you can use a still photographer to be on location, something we could not afford.) Many of the shots I would like to have considered were not useable because they were not in sharp focus and usually the lighting was not as I would like for poster art.

As it turned out, Angel did not have a poster company that we could use so I began my own search. I got proposals from several companies in Los Angeles but couldn't settle on one for either of two reasons. Some were outrageously expensive. Those that were not seemed to produce posters that all had a similar style. I was unsure that I could find someone both affordable and creative but kept looking. Meanwhile, I considered a very inexpensive option.

One of the actors who appeared in the movie was also a graphic artist. I thought he might be highly motivated to produce a poster that would be good, given his tie to the film. He agreed to try his hand at it but wanted some input such as images and text, which I gave. He produced exactly what I had suggested, which was totally no good. Just to check that instinct, I posted it on the Facebook page I had put up for the cast and crew. As expected, the comments were not favorable. The only positive outcome of the exercise was to teach me that I really needed to hire an experienced expert.

While the search for a poster artist was underway, I also started looking for a trailer maker. I first asked Charles, my editor, what he would charge for making one. But my experience with the poster and trying to do it "non-professionally" had made me wary.

After interviewing a couple of trailer houses in Los Angeles, I was unimpressed. They not only wanted fees that were out of range, they seemed bored with the prospect of working on a trailer for an indie. I decided to look and see what companies might be available in New York or even London.

I came across a firm named Giaronomo Productions, a movie advertising agency whose trailers online I really liked. After getting their price, however, I asked them if they could suggest someone more in my price range. To my great delight they helped me out and pointed me to Wheelhouse Creative in New York.

Hiring Wheelhouse

In early December, I talked with Wheelhouse and they were able to give me a package deal to do both the poster and trailer at a price I could manage. What a great break it was to get a company that turned out to be everything I could wish for. They were professional, creative, easy to work with, and on time with their products. Later, when I had a couple of glitches, they solved my problems.

The creative process working with Wheelhouse was a lot of fun. The person assigned to do the trailer came up with some ideas that not only captured the action in the film, but also the romance and humor. There was really only one quibble.

At the start of the trailer, he wanted to put one of the aerial views taken from the drone that just showed trees. I had put it in the film to capture the sense of place being in a nice neighborhood, but I didn't see why it was in the trailer, which had to be really short duration. I asked that it be taken out.

Interestingly, I got pushback. Zac Castellano, the artist from Wheelhouse doing the trailer, said that it had production value. He couldn't capture the fact of there being many interesting locations and a variety of camera angles with the footage that he needed to use to show basic plot themes. He insisted on keeping the aerial view at the start.

His perspective was valuable to me and I saw his point after the explanation. I had a brief thought: wouldn't it have been wonderful to have him on the filming team?

The poster was done by a different artist, Michael Boland. He asked for the stills that I would like him to consider using for the artwork. I sent him a few and we discovered that I was cutting images from the wrong version of the film. I needed to send him 4K, a much higher resolution. The problem then was that getting 4K stills required the additional step of my getting Charles to cut them for me and getting the exact second that he was to capture. It was really time-consuming to get the exact frame that would have the highest clarity.

Michael and I agreed that the poster should feature the Woman In Black. I kept looking for the right image and didn't find anything that made him say, "Ooh, that's it!" After going through numerous possibilities from the actual film, I went through some scenes and takes that we hadn't used in the movie and found a good candidate. It worked. It became the image that Michael projected onto a red background, which I thought was an absolutely brilliant decision.

When the poster was finished, the work was technically not over. Later it became necessary to resize the poster for a print copy, for a revamped Blu-Ray cover, as well as to create a horizontal version as required by Amazon. Although I am fairly proficient at working with Photoshop and layers, my efforts to rework the poster always had errors or impossible hurdles. I went back to Michael hat-in-hand a number of times and he was always good spirited about helping.

The day that I had both the poster and the trailer ready was pretty special. I uploaded the poster to the Pono Productions website and put the trailer on YouTube. Over the next months, the trailer got several hundred views. I was a little sad when the counter got reset to zero when the film finally went up on Amazon.

Composers

Although Angel and I talked about music, we couldn't make any progress on the subject. From my point of view, that was because he wanted to hire a music supervisor, which had never been budgeted for and now the money for such was impossible. So, I decided to move forward on this alone. I would select a composer and do all of the "supervision," including the selection of source music and contracting, myself.

A composer had read about our call for crew on the Internet and emailed me, asking if he could audition to be composer for the film. He asked if he could send me some sample music themes to show me his style. Thinking there'd be no harm in reviewing his work, I accepted. Because I liked what he sent, I let him read the script. He conveyed excitement about the project and wanted to pursue some trial ideas. Praise for the script, my baby, had the usual effect on me: I liked the people who admired it.

When he sent me some themes based on his reading of the script, I was less enthusiastic than when I'd first listened to his samples. When I was up-front with him about this, he asked for more details on what I was looking for. I told him my ideas. This is where I erred—not in what I did, but the way I did it.

Because I didn't want to hurt his feelings, I said that what he'd done was good, but that it needed work. What I should have said is, "This isn't what I am looking for. But if you want another chance, feel free to send me another iteration." Instead, I unthinkingly led him to believe that we were beginning a relationship and that he had what it would take, we just needed to hone it.

Later, when I told him I'd chosen another composer and thanked him for the time he'd spent applying for the job, he was furious. He said he wouldn't have wasted his time had he known there was another composer under serious consideration. I felt pretty down about it and vowed I must not let anyone else labor under the illusion that I was more interested in them than I really was.

As mentioned earlier, I liked Kays Al-Atrakchi's work very much. I called him to talk in more detail and was delighted with his proposed direction for music, his experience, and his attitude. We finalized the contract and signed it on November 8, 2016. Never once was I sorry I chose him and repeatedly I was glad. I give Zubi Mohammad full credit for finding the composer for the movie.

Kays had a limited time window to work on the film because he was booked for other projects in the spring of 2017. I felt a lot of pressure to get an early edit of the movie finished by mid-November, not only because Angel kept telling me that it should only take that long, but also, I wanted Kays to have something to work on as soon as possible.

Yet, my progress in editing was very slow from the beginning. I had a big problem: as noted, I didn't want to cut actors' airtime. And I didn't want to take out footage that was good because of artistry or production value, but which did not fit the overall emerging path of the movie. And I didn't want to hurt anyone's feelings. I was stuck. It was like having writer's block in the middle of drafting a novel.

At this point, I had a very crucial unplanned conversation with Kays. On a cold day I was sitting in my car in a parking lot outside a restaurant when I called him to tell him that the edit I planned to send him would be delayed. I confessed my hesitations I felt about cutting, the fear of hurting people. I withheld nothing, including my sense of isolation, and my fervent love of the movie and all its parts.

Kays graciously spent over an hour talking with me to get across a key notion: I needed to do what was for the good of the film, not what was good for any single actor or set of actors. Actors, he said, ultimately wanted to be in a great film, regardless of how much they appeared in it. Yes, they would like to be maximally seen, but it was more important to them that the film be a success. If the film were not good, and not a success, the amount they appeared on-screen wouldn't matter much. And then he said something else very important. He told me that I could do it and that it was obvious that I could. I just needed to knuckle down and make decisions wisely. He urged me to set aside the criticisms of others and let my creativity focus. "It is in there, you just need to let it out," I heard.

That pep talk was seminal. Having someone whom I respected tell me I could do it was a spur that countered the effects of others who kept telling me I couldn't do it. I went back to the drawing board and re-outlined how I wanted the film to proceed, how each character was supposed to play, and where I wanted fast versus slower pace. This allowed me to cut any scene, take, or sequence where someone was out-of-character. It made me ruthless in cutting parts that were not in focus, poorly conceived, or inconsistent with the storyline.

I continued to rely on Kays off and on for the remainder of the editing process. I called him a few more times with specific questions, and sometimes when I wanted his creative input. He was always positive. He was always ready to share his vast experience in a constructive way and didn't get angry when I didn't always take his advice. But often I did, and he had a strong impact on the film overall, particularly in two ways: making sure things appeared logical, especially after explanatory elements were cut; and, reorienting the focus of the film. Let me give but two examples.

Kays called one day to say that there was a logical inconsistency that needed fixing. The scene to which he was referring was one in which Marilyn Cummins is instructed by the police to wait in a car outside of her house while the police go inside to make sure the bad guy isn't there. Marilyn suddenly notices the bad guy's car parked nearby and loudly honks the horn of the car she's in to alert the police inside.

Kays pointed out that if the police were to hear the horn, which they would, then the logical thing for them to do is to come outside to help her. There is no way they would say to themselves, "Oh, she is honking because the bad guy's car is parked outside, and she wants to alert us that he is probably in here with us."

I immediately saw Kays' point. If the police were to do the logical thing and come outside, it would mess up the next events in which the police encounter the villain. This meant that they had to stay in the house. In other words, I needed to omit the honking that would logically bring them outside.

Another time, fairly early on in the editing, Kays phoned to talk about whether we should have a male or female sing the theme song. I didn't even pause, "Male." This led to a discussion as to how the actors had played their roles and how the director had directed them. The acting and the direction determined which characters were strongest and who dominated in each of the scenes.

Kays said, "You may have written this script with its being all about the woman protagonist, but do you think that is the way it evolved?" (Kays often asked questions that led my thinking rather than telling me conclusions or options outright.)

"No," I replied, "the way it is played by the actors as well as strength of the best scenes has made it as much his story as hers."

There was a brief silence before he said, "I totally agree. Now you need to let yourself edit for that."

Source Music

One of my early discussions with Kays was about source music. Although it was clear to me that certain types of music fit some scenes, there was also a lot of leeway in what to choose. Kays helped narrow the selection criteria. For example, we agreed that there should be country music playing in the gun shop scene. When I told Kays I preferred a female singer there, he said, "Look for a female Hank Williams," so I did.

I scoured the Internet looking for Texan female country singers with a perfect, polished voice and style. I finally found her—Kayla Ray. I loved her from the start. I sent a sample to Kays and he was equally impressed. But how to find her? I sent an email to her website contact form, to which there was no response.

As I waited to hear from Kayla, I turned to finding other source music. I tried to figure out how could I narrow the huge number of musicians down to those who'd be interested in trading their inclusion in the movie for use of their tunes. In a huge stroke of good fortune, the answer was provided by our drone pilot.

Sparky Sorenson, drone pilot extraordinaire, used to be a country music artist. As a result, he was familiar with a wide range of Texas bands and solo artists. He offered to send out an email to his contacts asking for interested people to send me some of their audio files. The response was amazing. I had dozens and dozens of wonderful musicians to choose from, all of whom were interested in the trade I had offered.

But Kayla Ray was not among them. I asked Sparky to try to locate her, so he did. And she said, "Yes." I was overjoyed. I asked Kayla if I could use a specific song of hers that I liked. She demurred that it was co-written with a former boyfriend who would probably not assent to using it. She suggested another song which was very suitable. I decided to push my luck and ask if I could use two of her songs, not knowing where the other would fit, but knowing I would find a place because I liked her sound so much. She agreed.

Then I began my review of the musicians who'd emailed me per Sparky's request. I tried to match songs and instrumentals to individual scenes in my mind, and then would email Kays my suggestions. In some cases, it was easy. The opening notes of Shaun Outen's "Señoritas and Tequila" were an instant match to the bar scene with one of the villains. In other cases, I agonized and took weeks to decide which song would fit where. And, ultimately, there were some source-music needs for which I had no musicians yet.

One example was the scene in the apartment of the detective who was from Hawai'i. From the 13 years I'd lived on Kaua'i, I knew there were some fabulous ukulele players and I really wanted to showcase ukulele music, which can be so much more complex than the simple chords most people associate with it. So, I returned to the Internet to look for just the right instrumental.

The first one I found was ideal, but the musician had the lackadaisical attitude of "I'll do it tomorrow" that used to drive me crazy when I lived in Hawai'i. It would take him days to answer an email. I decided to keep looking.

The second musician I found was a young man, Andrew Molina, who was willing for me to use his music, but told me that I had to go through his dad, who would handle everything. That turned out to be great because his father was business-minded, and we soon had agreement to use two of Andrew's instrumentals.

One of the most unusual pieces we used as source music was by Fredrick Chopin. Kays came up with the idea for it in the art gallery scene. He arranged and performed it, and it suits the scene very well.

The final example of source music that required more time than I'd expected was the song for the taco shop. Kays suggested an upbeat, Mariachi sort of song. When I kept running into obstacles finding someone local and who could speak English, I finally asked one of our Spanish-speaking cast members for help. He sent me some songs by a couple of his friends, and one was just right. Negotiating the contract was a bit of a juggle, but one of the musicians' wives had enough English to help close the deal.

Selecting the source music took many, many hours of work that was mostly fun. The parts that were not so enjoyable were preparing a template for the License Agreement, sending it to my attorney for comment, getting it signed by everyone, and obtaining information about royalties. Those tasks were pretty time-consuming. Through it all, I was lucky to have an interested and helpful partner, Kays.

Chapter 20: Sound

Although a Sound Designer would not be able to work on the film until we had finished editing it, I wanted to book one early so that I could be sure they would be available when I needed them. Also, I wanted to get the recruitment, contract, and budgeting activities out of the way before editing began.

Hiring Johnny Marshall

As with many subjects, I was a novice when it came to sound design. Yes, I knew that films need a sound designer to have the right noise when a door closes, a foot steps, or pencil taps. But I hadn't really thought of the importance of timing: the light switch needs to click exactly with the first frame of light coming on; or of tenor: the voice on the phone needs to be just so deep; or of small extraneous noises: the man with a slashed windpipe makes small guttural gasps. There is also the quality and nature of the sound. For example, a footstep is different when it is on concrete versus wood or gravel, etc. Nor had I fully appreciated the standards for clarity. It is essential that any dialog that is unclear either have additional dialog recorded or be cut.

Angel taught me that sound is a critical aspect of the film and that we needed to find the very best possible designer for the price we could pay. And I hoped, but didn't expect, that the someone would be local so that I could work with them in person. I was very excited at the notion learning of how sound is designed and getting to participate in the process.

The very first person we interviewed was someone who cost more than we'd budgeted (the ever-persistent problem) but was the right professional for the job in every other respect. He was Johnny Marshall.

To be truthful, I didn't have the expertise to judge his capabilities, but I could see from his resume that he'd done enough films, and high-level ones at that, to do a great job. So, what interested me was the individual.

I am a feelings person and my antennae are both long and sensitive. Johnny immediately struck me as being both relaxed in a hippie sort of way, and a highly demanding professional. What an interesting combination. Supple yet strong, quick but thorough, both staid and engaging.

Johnny had one more thing that was important to me: he was very enthusiastic about the screenplay. After he had read it, he told me that once he started it, he couldn't put it down. It was a true page-turner with an edginess that was both realistic and engaging. Then he stroked my ego by saying that he was not given to flattery, but that he found it remarkable that it was my first and only screenplay. He said the script really made him want to work on the movie, even though he had a lot of work lined up and did not need to take on anything extra at the time.

I knew that I would do whatever I needed to do budget-wise to get Johnny onto the movie. But it took me quite some doing to find the resources to hire him; I really was at the bottom of the barrel financially. I was overjoyed to sign the contract with him on November 7.

Sound Run Through

Johnny had a time window in the spring of 2017 that he had set aside for *Revenge In Kind*. I needed to meet that deadline or risk losing him, but I was behind with the editing. To make the schedule work, we decided to break the film into four reels so that there could be a portion of the movie he, as well as Kays, could get started on. Once Charles, Justin, and I finished a reel, it was locked. Although there were inevitable errors, we refrained from making any changes that would affect the timing of the movie and thus its music and other sound.

When we had finally finished all of the reels and the movie was in the hands of Kays and Johnny, there was no real break in the pace of work for me. But there was a new adventure—looking at the movie not from the perspective of its visual value, but in terms of its sound.

Johnny's sound studio was in a converted garage at his home. At the front of the studio was a big screen on which he would project the movie while designing the sound with a large keyboard in the center back of the room. On either side of his console were a small table and chair for observers such as me. I would sit at one of the tables and wear headphones as we went through the movie very slowly and carefully, with me listening to each of the sound sets he had designed.

One of the objectives I had for the sound was to make it easy for people with hearing impairment to hear voices without competition from background noise. This meant that the music, for example, had to be kept at a lower volume. There were other similar tweaks as well. I recall that at one point, Johnny had noticed a sound lull and thus introduced a dog barking in the background. Because the dog logically would not just stop when dialog restarted, the barking intermittently continued. I told Johnny that to someone with hearing aids, like me, the barking was interfering with understanding what was being said, so he adjusted both the volume and the location of the barking sound.

Another example was telephones ringing in the background of the police squad room. To reduce the sound competition, Johnny changed the ring tone of the phones and lowered the number and changed the timing. He made similar adjustments throughout the movie as I listened and told him where my poor hearing made background noise a hindrance. In my opinion, every movie should have a hearing-impaired person go through the sound with the designer to make audibility easier.

One interesting fact to me was how sound has to be precise to the split second. For example, in one scene someone turns on a light. Johnny had put in the click of the light switch, but it seemed a bit off from when the light came on. The difference was minuscule, but noticeable when you are going slowly through the film looking for any errors. He slowed down the movie to the exact frame where the light can first be detected and moved the initiation of the click by a fraction of a second to that location. Maybe no one would have noticed the difference, but that was the level of detail we were working at.

Additional Dialog Recording

One of the mistakes I made in drafting contracts was actually a deletion rather than an omission. Angel told me, "We will never have the money to do ADR [additional dialog recording], so take that out of the actors' contracts." (He was trying to make sure the contracts were as simple and short as possible.)

I understood that ADR was done when the voices recorded lacked necessary clarity, but I didn't have a solid appreciation of what all can cause the problem. Well, it turns out to be any number of things, including machine noises, mistakes by the sound man, an inoperable boom, or a problematic microphone. But I learned all of that in retrospect, after the film was shot. Not knowing it in advance, I took out of the contract that actors would have to do ADR. That was a mistake.

As it turned out, we had very substantial problems with sound. There was an entire sequence shot in a car that took the better part of a day to film. The camera work wasn't very good, but it was useable. Yet the audio was so awful it was unusable. I really wanted to keep the scene because the dialog was important, but not integral, to the plot. And the banter between the characters helped develop their relationship. To boot, the imagery out the windows revealed Dallas and had good production value. Well, because of the bad sound, the car scene went out the editing window.

There were other sound issues as well, including humming machines that couldn't be turned off, a dysfunctional microphone in a murder scene, and voices drowned out by a passing vehicle. There was also absence of key human noises in a host of scenes such as the victim praying, a dying man choking, a woman pleading, and a voice over the telephone. These crucial sound requirements necessitated ADR.

I tried to do as much of the ADR as I could myself to keep from having to bring people in to do it. It turned out to be a lot of fun. I made several recordings—choking noises for the dying, the whispers of prayer, and the telephone voice of the 911 operator. Johnny manipulated these recordings to make them fit the circumstances. For example, he lowered the tone of my voice so that it sounds like a male speaking on the phone.

The way ADR works is that the relevant scene is projected on the screen while the speaker stands in front of a microphone with a headset on. You hear three clicks and then the film rolls. You watch the lips of the person onscreen, or the action you need to match, to synch your speech with the movement. For some people, this is as easy as bouncing a ball; for others, it takes many repetitions.

For some of the places we needed ADR, it was not required that the person doing the sound be the same as the person who is visually in the film. I toyed with the idea of getting some friends to come in and ADR some of these voices that we needed. But then it occurred to me that the extras who played the roles might enjoy the ADR process and learn from it as well. I decided to forthrightly ask them if they'd like to do it for free, with the understanding that there was no obligation or pressure. They all jumped at the chance. After all, having not only your visage, but your voice, in a movie is great fun.

A rather humorous thing happened in regard to the extras. A very tall, hefty man played the medical examiner. The trouble was that there were two extras' names by the role in the log. So, I called the first guy on the list and asked him if he had played the medical examiner and he replied yes.

When we opened the studio door to let him in, it was not the big man who played the medical examiner at all; it was a small, slim fellow with a decidedly wrong voice for the man playing the role. Not wanting to offend him since he'd shown up, and not being sure we would get someone with the right voice, we let him do the ADR. Afterward I was able to reach the person who'd really played the role and he came gladly to do the ADR as well.

In cases where a voice already known to the audience was needed, we had to bring in the relevant actors. We had to bring in both Chad Halbrook and Chester Gayao to ADR a few scenes. Getting ADR for Sasha Higgins, who lives in LA, was more difficult. Eventually we found an affordable sound designer near LA who was able to get us a quality product.

After we finished ADR, the sound was done. Johnny did a final run-through with me in his studio, then said we needed to hear it in a theater. He arranged through an acquaintance of his to use the Texas Theater, which is cavernous.

With just the two of us in the theater, the sound was very hard for me to hear, but Johnny had no problem. What thrilled me was to see it on a huge screen.

When we finished watching, Johnny said, "It is all done. I didn't see or hear any problems." Wow, what a moment.

Friendly Help

Looking back, there is another note I would like to add about Johnny. He was a fount of knowledge about film and helped me with issues that transcended sound. Let me give an example.

Midway through our sound work, I mentioned a concern of mine to Johnny as I stood to leave at the end of one of our meetings. I told him that I was struggling with the start of the film. It seemed slow and did not grip the viewer, although it was chronologically correct. I told him I didn't know how to fix it.

He replied that the script was creepy and that the start of the movie should establish that. He said that the scene where Lehman shaves his body—to assure that he leaves no hair at the scene of his crimes— comes several scenes into the movie. Johnny said the scene is full of evil, so ominous, that maybe I should move it up begin the movie with that. It was a stroke of genius and creativity and I give him full credit not only for the idea, but for being willing to help me with film issues across the board.

K. C. Bailey

Chapter 21: Coloring

I am a professional photographer who takes color extremely seriously. This is perhaps why one requirement for *Revenge In Kind* was crystal clear for me from the outset: I didn't want a dark or unnaturally hued film. The film would not be de-saturated, heavily contrasted, or look as if shot through a colored lens. I conveyed this to everyone relevant right from the start, particularly the director, cinematographer, and digital imaging technician (DIT). Anyone who did not fulfill these coloring objectives would at some point be overruled.

During pre-production (the week before filming was to start), I met at the camera rental office with Laurel Warren, the DIT, her husband Justin Warren (who would be our Colorist, but who was also a DIT), Roger, and our cinematographer. We were picking up the "Red" camera and going over some coloring questions. I told everyone (again) my desire not to have a dark movie and, as we were cycling though some color on the computer, expressed opinion about what hues I preferred. Apparently, my expression of opinion was an unexpected interference to some.

Later, Roger called me to say that the cinematographer was extremely upset because it is not industry standard to have the executive producer (me) decide on coloring or related issues. I reminded him that I had been clear in my interviews of everyone that I would be determining such and that it was even in each contract that I would reserve final artistic control. He replied that coloring could be "fixed" in post-production, so I could go easy during the filming. He wanted me to give some free rein to the cinematographer to keep her happy, and to have my input to her go through him. I agreed.

So, during production, I said no more to the cinematographer about much of anything, but I let the DIT know that I would be making the coloring decisions during post-production. Laurel fully understood that it was my film, my choice.

The Coloring Process

When finally the film was fully edited four months after shooting, it was time to do the color. I had selected Justin Warren as my colorist for several reasons. His reputation and credentials were superb, I liked him the moment I met him, his wife (our DIT) was a fabulous person, Angel recommended him highly, and he lived in Ft. Worth. This meant that I could go and personally work with him on the film. I can honestly say that my coloring experience with Justin was nothing short of exceptional. He is highly creative and knowledgeable.

When I met Justin at his studio, there was an edge to him. As I have said, I can sense emanations from another person, and I know when the creative spirit of a person occasionally overtakes them like night does day. I felt that Justin was an artist whose creative genius could result in highs and lows. He was extremely self-assured, yet full of doubt—that potent mix that can result in fine art as well as moodiness. And his pursuit of the ultimate in his art made him open to any credible (in his demanding and restricted definition) creative input. I was fortunate to earn his respect and trust, and that we became a team.

One of the first questions Justin asked me was whether I understood that there was a disconnect between my preferences for color and those that had been developed during filming. He said the cinematographer preferred that the film have a darker, somewhat bluish hue.

I explained that I was paying for the entire movie and that I intended to supervise the coloring the way I wanted it. Justin understood my position and was glad that I had clear ideas about the way I wanted the film to look. So, we dove right in.

I went to Justin's studio every workday and some weekends for a couple of months for about 6 hours a day. We would watch each scene and discuss what, if anything, needed changing. And there were a huge number of changes. A usual problem was skin color, which was fairly easy to adjust. And there were a host of situations where the coloring needed changing due to imbalance. For example, an extra's clothing would rivet the eye, but de-saturating it made it innocuous.

Then there were what I think of as "middle" problems, ones that took some time to fix, but which were not as challenging as the "bad" issues. Many of these resulted from odd lighting. For example, one of the first scenes in the movie is in a bedroom. The light from one lamp was warm and from the other, cool. And one was brighter than the other. The adjustments had to be made not only to the lamps, but the areas onto which they cast light. If I had the movie to do over again, I would make sure that every lamp has the same type of warmth and that each be put on a rheostat.

Really Hard Problems

There were two sets of problems that were very time-consuming to fix. The first involved some scenes with backlighting and which were improperly exposed and poorly shot. These required that Justin go through and "tint" the background frame-by-frame because actors were moving and continually exposing the brightness behind them.

To understand what I mean, imagine someone standing in front of a wall with a light shining on them so that a shadow is cast directly behind them. Then imagine that the person moves, but the shadow does not. That is akin to the problem Justin had to fix—to make the shadow move with the person and the background to turn white where the shadow had left.

One of the most difficult experiences of this "shadow" problem came from a scene in which Detective Coxon confronts Sarah Scott about whether she's the perpetrator. It is shot mostly with the two characters in front of a window that looks out on a spectacular view of the Dallas skyline. The overly bright backlighting had to be reduced frame by frame because of hand and head motions. It couldn't be automated because the motions would leave bright spots unless they were manually adjusted.

It was a very time-consuming process and more than a little frustrating to Justin. It became so complicated and such a time-sink that at one point I said that we should just forget it and let it be what it was. To his credit, Justin firmly said, "You don't want that kind of low quality in your film. We need to take the time to fix these problems." Thank goodness he exhibited extra patience when mine wore thin.

The second problem was over-lighting. The worst case was a house at night in one of the final scenes. It was like it had a set of searchlights on it—so unnaturally bright and unreal. It was difficult to fix because it entailed greying the light, which risked looking artificial. It still bothers me when I look at it, but it is much better than it would be if we'd left it alone.

In addition to the problem-fixing, there were the fascinating, creative aspects of coloring. Justin made sure, for example, that a gunshot flash cast just the right amount of light on the face of the shooter; that the movie being watched on an iPad by the bad guy reflected moving light just right on his face; that a flashlight shone down a hall appeared at the correct moment and intensity.

One of Justin's suggestions that I liked very much, and which we incorporated, was a tonal shift in tint when the lead actor comes to understand the magnitude of the problems he faces. The hue we used from this point forward is slightly yellowed and a bit de-saturated. I think it adds tremendously to the emotional shift of the viewer of the film, yet it is subtle enough to not be obvious.

The Bedroom Scene

One aspect of the bed scene that I like is what Justin did with it. The bedroom is white walled with grey carpet, black & white photos on the wall, and the sheets were black. Justin said, "What do you think about emphasizing the B&W nature of it by even removing a bit more of the color and maybe cooling down the light? It will almost be like this scene is shot in black and white."

"That's absolutely brilliant," I said, "let's do it!"

We spent two days on adjusting the color of that scene and it was hard work. For example, he would change the skin tones and light warmth, have me critique, and then readjust. It may sound odd, but it was almost as if my colorist and I were doing a sort of dance. We were very in synch, feeding off of one another.

A Calibration Issue

We were several days into the coloring process and almost a quarter of the way working through the film when Justin told me he had an offer to go and be DIT on a movie being shot in LA. He wanted to take five weeks off and do that film.

I was crestfallen, as I felt we were in a rhythm and I didn't want to break the creative continuity. But I knew this was a good opportunity for him, so I agreed.

When Justin returned, he said that while in LA he had discovered that his monitor was not correctly calibrated. With the corrected monitor, we looked at the coloring done before his departure and we could readily see at least one manifestation of the issue—the greens were way too intense and unrealistic. There were other problems too.

It took three days to redo the work that had already been done to correct for the calibration error. I was upset about it due to the financial cost to me, but I did not want to cause a rift by arguing over money, so I ate it.

Making a Body Dead

A dead body is not just a still body, it has a certain color. Not colorlessness, color. If you have seen one, depending on the length of time since death, it has a progression of losing (in the case of a Caucasian) pink and taking on grey. And there is almost an artificiality about it, as if the body never really lived. You can almost imagine that someone took away the carcass that used to be living and replaced it with a less-than-adequate substitute that is somehow not quite right. Without the life of the person that once inhabited it, the body loses more than the life it held; it loses its realism.

So often movies do not capture the appearance of death, particularly in the case of murders. The film may portray a body that is bloody, but that blood appears applied rather than shed; the body may be still, but not obviously absent spirit; it may be laid out, but lacks the seeming obscenity that accompanies one who is splayed ignominiously after having been felled.

Filming An Indie

I wanted the death of the young girl in the movie to be portrayed in a way that would capture the horror, sadness, and unfairness of murder. So many things had to come together just right to make that happen. The actress had to be willing to act, purely act. In other words, she had to abandon any attempt to "look good" and allow herself to be what she was—murdered.

Roger had to position her on the bed in a convincing manner. The male on-looking actors had to be totally professional, because one simple jocular remark could have marred the seriousness with which the scene was laid out and played, and thus how it would appear on screen. And the camera work had to be exceptional, with the angle capturing the scene without being prurient or grotesque.

When I first viewed the takes of the death scene, I was silent and sad. It was that good. I stared for a long time, thinking of just how much time would be on the body, and then on the action around the body. The balance needed to be just right. Enough on her to show that the scene was ever so serious, yet enough on the investigators to keep the action moving and the dialog relevant. It took a lot of thought and time, but in the end, it felt right.

But it had to wait until coloring to make the scene whole. By that I mean that during editing the "dead" body was still pink, still alive.

When Justin and I got to the death scene, we spent a lot of time analyzing it. I was the one who knew what hue of grey we were after for the body, so we worked until we got that. But we also needed to subdue the other colors in the room as well as the lighting. It had to inter-mesh.

In the end, we achieved a color correction for the scene that I think goes very well with the somberness of murder, with the loss of a young life. The effect on the viewer is subtle, but that is the way it should be. No one should know that the mood is being set for them by light and color; it should just happen.

But all of that effort at making sure that death is properly conveyed almost went for naught. It was during the final sound design review, after the coloring had been completed, when Sound Designer Johnny Marshall said, "Hey, are you going to fix the heart throb?"

"What heart throb?" I asked.

"You know, María De La Cruz. When she is lying there dead, you can see the blood pulsing in her neck."

Shit. I hadn't seen it. My editor hadn't seen it. My colorist hadn't seen it.

I went back to Justin after we'd finished coloring. "Hey, let's fix the heart throb."

That really unnerved me. If I had missed that, what other obvious things had I missed? It is okay if I saw something and chose not to fix it or couldn't fix it. But the throb was in a scene for which I had pulled out all of the stops on the amount of time and level of attention I'd been willing to devote to getting it right.

But, thanks to all those who put so much into making that scene, I think it came off very well. And, thanks to Johnny, it wasn't blown by having the stupid mistake of a pulse.

Treating Myself

The coloring was slower-paced than any of the other film-related activity so far, primarily because I had to leave Justin's house by mid-afternoon in Ft. Worth to get home in time to do Pono's insulin by 5:00 PM. That meant that I had more time for myself, which I used to research various neurological disorders. I was looking for anything that would explain my condition.

In early May 2017, I came across an article on the Internet entitled "Cysteine, Sulfite, and Glutamate Toxicity: A Cause of ALS?[1]" This interested me because I knew that I was allergic to sulfa drugs and eggs (the yolks of which contain high levels of sulphur) as well as vaccines produced from eggs. I also knew that I had a sensitivity to monosodium glutamate; I would get restless leg syndrome whenever I ate food containing it. Could it be that my neurological reactions were due to an allergy?

---

[1] Patricia B.E. Woolsey, The Journal of Alternative and Complementary Medicine, Volume 14, Number 9, 2008, pp. 1159-1164.

Filming An Indie

After doing further research on diet and sulfites, the obvious lightbulb went on. I had been drinking copious amounts of sulfite-laden wine every single day and, very often, consuming dried fruits preserved with sulfites. I decided that I absolutely had to change this to see if the problem would resolve.

On May 11, 2017, I went cold turkey on wine. This took almost more will power than I had. In my apartment, I had several cases of wine, but I succeeded in not touching it anymore—not one glass, not one sip. I considered my condition to be so dire that it was worth the sacrifice to do the experiment. (I switched to scotch but limited my intake of that as well in case the issue was also alcohol consumption.) I kept a written log about my condition to track if there were any success.

On May 14, I had the first night of no cramps in my feet and legs for over eight months. I also noticed remarkable improvement in the fasciculations. Although I still had many nights and days that the problems manifested, my condition improved markedly. Then I tried to start being equally careful about glutamate as well. That had no effect, but I continued it nonetheless.

In the summer of 2017, I had improved to the extent that I felt that I might be able to sleep without the CPAP. I tried it and was no longer waking up gasping for breath.

As of this writing in 2020, I still suffer from leg and foot cramps a few times a week, but no longer daily, and the fasciculations have all but disappeared. There are still times when my hands misbehave and I am unable to write or type all day, but the frequency of this occurrence is greatly reduced.

Although I still miss drinking wine because I loved it so, there is no way I will ever go back to it. There may be something else wrong with me neurologically, but I am now certain that the sulfites played a key role in my problems.

The change in my health was radical, as was the impact of the change on my psychology. I had been living life as if it would be curtailed at any moment. Now that I no longer believed I had ALS, and no longer thought I was destined to die within months, everything changed. In most regards, it was wonderful. It was like casting off heavy chains. It was also somewhat scary in a very, very different way: now I would be facing my future without a lifetime's savings.

Chapter 22: What To Do With The Movie

One of the hopes I had from the outset of making the movie was to subtitle it in a few other languages. When I looked online in early 2016 for companies that could provide this service for an independent movie, I could not find any options. Subtitles could wait, however, as there were many things that could still derail the film from being completed at all.

In October 2016, when we finally completed production, I looked simultaneously into three options: festivals, turning the film over to a distributor, and selling it myself on disc or via streaming. Also, regardless of what manner the film was presented to the public, I knew I still wanted to subtitle it in French, Spanish, and Japanese if I could afford it.

Festivals

Angel had asked me soon after we met what I wanted to do with the movie once it was made. I said without much forethought that wanted to enter it into film festivals. He explained that festivals were not a merit-based process and that I would probably need to know someone on the inside to get an invitation.

Although I knew no one on the inside or who could introduce me to the right people, I took a chance and paid the fees to enter ten festivals. Once you enter, your film is vetted, competes against other films, and then invited or not. Ultimately, *Revenge In Kind* was rejected by all.

It really surprised me that the film did not make it into a single festival, so I wanted to know more about the selection process. I called a woman associated with a New York festival who explained it to me. She said there was an initial selection panel, usually comprised of young, low-paid people with little or no film training, who viewed the first few minutes of a film to decide whether it would go on to the next stage to be viewed more thoroughly. This first panel would receive instructions such as: "No violence against women." Or "No kinky sex." Or whatever. The job of these kids was only to look for the no-noes on their checklist.

In the case of *Revenge In Kind*, the New York woman told me, there is violence against a woman in the first few minutes of the movie. This, in our current times, is not something most festivals want, she said. There is no way your movie would make it past the reviewers for most festivals.

The woman also told me that even if *Revenge In Kind* had made it through the initial panel selection process, it would be competing with scores of films for one of only a few slots because most of the movies for the festival would have already been chosen by prior arrangement with a studio, a friend of the festival, or other inside connection.

If I had known beforehand what the New York festival woman told me, I would never have wasted the money applying for so many festivals. Instead, I would have worked hard to focus on only a couple in order to try and gain an inside track to assure an invitation, or at least a fair chance at one.

Aside from the lost entry fees, there was another major downside to my having tried the festival route—time lost. Almost every festival requires that a film not have been shown publicly yet, and the time from entry to the contest to hearing the results is on average 3 months. To keep from violating that no-public-viewing restriction, I withheld the film from distribution for 6 months, from May 2017, when it was finished, to October 2017.

The Distribution Racket

Angel also had told me to be cautious about distributors because they usually will take your film, make money on it, and assure that you get almost nothing in return.

So, I took special care to research on the Internet about others' experiences with distributors to help avoid the pitfalls.

I learned that distributors' main ploy is to promise a return of a goodly profit minus specified marketing costs. And it is the marketing costs that guarantee that you'll never see any money. This warning about the never-ending marketing is widely documented on the Internet, but I also heard about it from a few filmmakers who'd experienced it. Nevertheless, I decided to try to get a distributor and hoped that my wariness would help protect me from a bad deal.

Several people had suggested that I attend the annual American Film Market (AFM) in Los Angeles where you can pitch your film to a large number of distributors. I had made my hotel and air reservations six months in advance and began the process of contacting distributors to ask for appointments at AFM.

One company responded right away, requesting that I not wait until AFM and that I sign a contract with them immediately. Their marketing to me was pretty high-pressure, saying that it was a now-or-never deal that would not be open to me for long. I asked for the contract to read the fine print.

What I saw was what I had been warned about. The contract provided that I would pay for publicity, any necessary re-branding, updates of artwork, and other marketing functions. When I asked if there were data available on the average cost of these services, I was told that they vary too widely for an average to be useful. When I asked if there would be a cap on such expenditures, the answer was that they would not exceed by much the film's earnings.

After several emails and telephone conversations, I decided to pass on the opportunity. Because this company had been one of the best-looking ones of the roster of distributors that attend AFM, I began to question my own attendance. Ultimately, I decided not to go and opted to go with my fallback plan for self-distribution instead.

Distribber

In 2016, it was not possible for an independent filmmaker to prepare and directly upload films to online platforms (e.g., iTunes, GooglePlay, and Amazon). [In 2019,

Amazon began a service which allows filmmakers to upload films themselves.] At the time, one had to rely on an aggregator to provide this service. I found Distribber, which had an excellent webpage and one of the most skilled hucksters I ever encountered.

The guy who marketed Distribber promised that his company, for a set flat fee, would place *Revenge In Kind* on 3 platforms of my choice, would do a quick and thorough quality control check first, and arrange for both closed captions and subtitles in whatever foreign languages I chose. He portrayed his company as skilled, efficient, and experienced. My project would be assigned a manager, who would be available to me whenever I needed to make any technical adjustments or answer any questions. That manager would subcontract for subtitles as soon as I signed with Distribber.

Everything he told me sounded really good, but just to make sure, I asked Angel to have a telephone conference call with the Distribber representative to make sure that Angel thought it was a good deal too. After Angel interviewed him with me and gave his thumbs up, I eagerly signed the Distribber agreement.

The first signs of trouble were when I tried to order subtitles. I kept getting put off, with my Distribber "personal manager" telling me that there were delays in getting responses from subcontractors. While the effort to contract out for subtitles languished, there were several technical glitches in getting the film ready to load up to the platforms. I grew weary of trying to get in touch with my manager and not getting clear or prompt answers. I was sorry that I had selected Distribber.

Finally, in frustration with non-delivery and non-communication, I terminated my contract with Distribber in August 2017. Although they had delivered nothing, Distribber refused to refund my money. Thankfully, I had paid my deposit of one-half the total fee to them using American Express and, after providing documentation of my case, was able to get my money back. [Two years later I learned that Distribber had gone bankrupt, leaving many independent films in the lurch.]

Obtaining Subtitles

The experience with Distribber's inability to provide subtitles led me to question whether it would be best to find a company that specializes in doing them. I did a bit of research online and found BTI Services, which provides subtitles for films among other things. Upon contacting them, I was immediately impressed. They told me: this is what we do, this is what it costs, this is when you will get the product, and this is how we guarantee our work. There was no high pressure. It was completely refreshing, and I decided to work with BTI. [BTI later became part of Iyuno Media Group.]

BTI was extraordinarily professional and responsive throughout my dealings with them. The subtitles in all three languages as well as subtitles for the deaf and hearing impaired in English were done within three months. There were no nasty surprises.

I did not understand that the subtitle files required for Blu-Rays, for DVDs, and for streaming film are all quite different. Thus I had to get three different file types—.stl, .png, and .itt. And for Japanese, the files needed to be son-tiff because the language uses pictographs.

At one point two years after post-production ended, I could not find some .stl files. I think they were on a G Drive that failed. At any rate, I contacted Iyuno and they still had them in the archive. They sent them to me the day after I requested them at no charge. I cannot praise the quality of this company highly enough. If you need subtitles done for your film, I recommend Iyuno.

Walla (Aka Mojo)

While BTI was working on subtitles, I resumed my search for another aggregator to perform the service of uploading film to streaming platforms. After looking at costs and promises from a few, I decided to try Juice Worldwide, which was given a "preferred plus" rating of aggregators by iTunes.

As soon as I had decided on Juice, there were similar technical and communications problems. I uploaded the film and audio assets, then began waiting. The quality control check was repeatedly delayed. Because the company's office was in Canada, I couldn't call them without increasing my telephone bill substantially, so I was trying to rely on email. My emails to the Juice project manager would take days to answer, if at all. Rather than waste months as I had with Distribber, I terminated with Juice.

In late September 2017, I then chose Walla, LLC (also listed online as Mojo) to get my film onto the streaming platforms. It also was listed by Amazon and iTunes as a "preferred aggregator." As with Distribber and Juice, the sales representative was excellent.

One of the interesting things that the sales rep for Walla offered was a service to make DVDs and Blu-Ray discs that could be sold on Amazon. I asked whether Walla made these in-house or subcontracted them. I noted that, as in the case of subtitles, subcontracting the work could lead to delays and quality problems. The representative answered that, yes, the work was subcontracted, but to a very reputable firm called Allied Vaughn. He said he would email me the price for adding on the disc production to the aggregator contract.

When I received the price for having discs made, it was hefty. I decided to check around to see what other companies would charge for the same service. I called four companies, all of which were much less expensive. I decided to contract with Walla only for the aggregator service.

Once the contract was signed with Walla, the follow through by non-sales staff was spotty and slow. Even though the film was supposed to take only 3 to 4 weeks to upload if there were no quality control issues (there weren't), it took until late November to complete the process. Nevertheless, the experience was better than I had encountered with Distribber and Juice.

Once Walla got my film onto the platforms I selected, it took them 6 months to begin reporting sales, which technically was a violation of the contract, but is apparently not unusual, particularly for iTunes. For a while, Walla made sales data available, but then stopped. They made payments in 2018 and early 2019, then stopped that too. When I tried to get them to give me sales data and payments, they quit responding to emails and phone calls. When I wrote the head of the company to complain of no payment or sales data, they blocked all emails coming from my computer.

In March 2020, I used the info@ email address on their website—the only way I could think of to reach them—to request termination of the contract and for the film to be taken down from all platforms. I also asked for sales data and past-due payments.

While they took the film down from the platforms, as of May 2020, they still have not provided complete sales data or paid sums owed.

Allied Vaughn

What to do with the film was an evolutionary process. Once it was clear that I could not easily find a distributor I could trust, the decision to self-distribute using an aggregator was the remaining choice. Likewise, when it was clear that using an aggregator to make discs was going to be significantly more costly than utilizing a specialty disc-maker for DVDs and Blu-Rays, it was clear that I would choose the disc-maker.

Before I could choose a disc-maker, I knew I would need a bar code. It would be less expensive if I were to obtain one myself rather than depending on the disc-maker to provide one.

Online, it was easy to locate GS1, a company that enables one to get a 10-digit number to use for my company in producing bar codes. For a fee, GS1 assigns your company a unique prefix. But creating the bar code with that number requires a bit of education. Fortunately, the website has a tutorial to walk you through the steps to creating the appropriate bar code for the type of product and packaging that you are going to use. This process was not particularly hard, but for me it was fairly time-consuming. When I finally got it right, it was time to select a disc-maker.

My plan, which was totally foolish, was to have a bunch of discs produced in hard copy mailed to me. Then I would sell them on Amazon myself. This would not only clutter my garage but would require me to do the mundane mailing and accounting. But at first, I did not think this out clearly. [Keep in mind that in 2017, disc manufacture-on-demand was just beginning to be readily available.]

I found a disc-maker in New Jersey that had good prices and a solid reputation, so I decided to work with them. It was a company that specialized not in feature films, but in discs for companies such as instructional or marketing videos. Thus, there were three limitations with this company that I did not appreciate at the outset.

The first problem we encountered was artwork for the DVDs versus the Blu-Rays. The artwork needed to be in two different formats and sizes, a service that this company was not able to provide. This meant that I would have to have it redone, which would take time and be more costly than just having someone who could manipulate the existing artwork to make it fit.

The second problem was that I needed a languages menu for the front of the film. I had failed to have this done when the film was being edited, so now I wanted to depend on the disc-maker to help me with inserting this at the front of the film.

The third was the most insurmountable; the formatting for the DVD is different from the Blu-Ray. The company I had chosen had only limited experience with Blu-Rays. There were technical issues early.

Both the company and I came to realize that the job I needed done was going to be difficult and perhaps impossible for them to perform well. We decided to part ways and they agreed to refund my deposit.

As I was discovering the three problems noted above, I began to try to find a company that specializes in discs specifically for movies. In the 2017 timeframe, there were none that presented themselves obviously as such on the Internet. However, I happened to recall the brief mention of the company Allied Vaughn in a phone conversation with the Walla salesman.

From their webpage, I was uncertain that Allied Vaughn provided what I was looking for, so I called them. After a few tries, I got through to someone who told me that indeed, they produce DVDs and Blu-Rays for sale and could put them on Amazon for me, using manufacture-on-demand. We discussed the three issues I had with the New Jersey disc-maker and they told me that those needs could easily be met.

Allied Vaughn provided everything promised. They are a highly reputable firm in my experience, and I am so glad that I went with them. They do manufacture-on-demand for over 10,000 movie titles and with mostly large studios, but my single indie has been treated with respect and care. Also, I get my sales data and payment on time.

Bitmax, et al

After the fiasco with Walla, I felt burned. Not only did they quit giving me sales data, they owed me [and still do] at least $650. So, I researched very carefully the companies that could put the film back up for streaming. I knew that I wanted to stream on iTunes, so I again looked at their list of "preferred aggregators."

There were nine companies listed by iTunes as preferred aggregators, including Juice Worldwide and Walla, with which I already had bad experiences. So that left seven. One firm was Japanese and worked with films in Asia only, another worked mostly in Russia and Eastern Europe, and another was in Hong Kong. I thought that I should try the Hong Kong one, Best & Original. The email was kicked back as undeliverable. That left four that were listed as working with or in the US.

I called the first on my list, Visual Data Media Services. I asked the man who answered the phone if he were the correct person to speak with about film aggregation services to iTunes. He replied, "What is film aggregation services?" I explained it to him, and he said, "I don't think we do that here." I asked him if he could pass along my contact information to whomever might be able to look into this in more detail. He agreed.

Later I got a call from a woman who said that she did not know the answer either, but that I would need to talk to their billing department. I asked why billing would be the right people to answer questions about aggregation services. Her answer did not make sense, so I just let that one go.

The next company I tried was Premier Digital. I got a recording and left a voicemail about what I wanted. I never got a call back.

At this point I had a thought: why not check to see if any of these companies has a Better Business Bureau rating? I checked and one of the two firms remaining on my list, Bitmax, had a positive BBB score. I decided to contact them next.

Chapter 23: The Final Product

When all of the editing, sound, and coloring were completed, I watched the movie straight through several times in a row. While I can truthfully say I thought the film was pretty darn good, I didn't feel it was as riveting as what had played in my head so many hours during the writing of the script and planning for the filming. What was missing, in my opinion, was the strength and slight wackiness of the protagonist, and the level of contempt and raw violence in her fights and the murder of a villain. Additionally, the admiring love of the detective for her was there during the course of the story, but it did not have the vibrant and consuming quality I had imagined, at least not until the end of the movie.

Some of the reasons that the movie did not have these elements were due to the problems described in this diary—problems that led to scenes being deleted or edited in a manner other than what I would have preferred. Another reason is, as noted earlier, it was acted and directed in a manner that made the story as much about the detective as it was about the police psychologist and underplayed the power of her personality.

Nevertheless, for a low-budget film that was confronted with endless challenges, I was very proud of the product. The more I look back on the process of making the film as I write this diary I realize that we all did a remarkable job to complete the project and to make it entertaining. I am someone who cuts short the viewing of any film that is not enjoyable. I have no problem watching *Revenge In Kind* all the way through repeatedly. Many other people have told me they found the movie captivating as well. The bottom line is that I would rate it much more highly than 75% of the independent movies I have seen.

The Digital Cinema Package

When the final-final of the film was completed in May 2017, I wanted to have a theater showing and invite all of the cast and crew. The public would not be invited so as to not violate the prohibition by most film festivals against public showings (prior to those festivals).

First, I needed to have a digital cinema package (DCP) created. This is a digital form of the film that can be ingested into the types of projectors available in most cinemas today.

Because at the time I still had high hopes that *Revenge In Kind* would be accepted at film festivals worldwide, I wanted to have four DCPs made. That turned out to be a $300 mistake because I ultimately only needed one.

It was of interest to me that the DCP is not a plug-and-play device. I had somehow envisioned it as being a hard drive that behaves somewhat like a Blu-Ray disc. Rather, the ingestion process takes hours and only when the movie is "unwound" into the projector is it available for showing.

The Cast & Crew Premiere

I wanted everyone who had participated in making the film to see it not only together as a group, but also to view it on a big screen the first time they saw it. Finding a place where I could do this affordably required a bit of searching. After contacting several theaters to get their prices, I settled on the Angelika Theater in Dallas.

For financial reasons, I had to rent the smallest of the several theaters in the building, which meant that I would have to restrict the number of accompanying family members of the cast and crew. That made me unhappy, but it was necessary.

When the manager of the Angelika learned that every seat in the house would be taken, he graciously offered me a free upgrade to the next capacity, to a 129-seat venue. This stroke of luck came only one day before the premiere, so it was too late for many of the cast and crew to be able to bring additional attendees. Although this meant that there would be some empty seats, at least everyone got to bring someone along if they wished.

The premier for cast and crew was held on June 7, 2017 at 6:30 PM. I arrived early and stood silently alone in the theater. Here, in just one hour, my film dream would be reality. It would be on a big screen and the very fact of that would be a closure of a huge journey.

After the crowd had taken their seats, I welcomed them and introduced some special guests. Not only had Lisa Fox of the hospital where we had filmed come to see the movie, but also a representative from the Mesquite Police Department.

Then I said a bit about post-production because most of the attendees knew nothing about what had happened with the movie since they had filmed it. Then I made introductions of the post-production team.

I had been afraid that I might forget someone, so I had written the names of those whom I wanted to introduce on my palm, which was covered in blue ink. Maybe no one thought it odd that I peered at my upheld hand at the end to make sure I had not missed any anyone.

I sat in the last row of the theater alone, so that I could watch the reactions of the audience. Once the movie began, it seemed to me that everyone was rapt. There was no talking and fidgeting.

When the movie was over, everyone cheered loudly. They really seemed to like it. I went to the front to tell people goodbye and to congratulate them on their parts in the process.

As everyone was filing out of the theater and a few cast and crew were taking selfies, Roger came to me and said that that the film turned out pretty well. I thanked him for that, and for being director. He then asked why I had not let him participate in the editing process. Because I didn't want to debate with him when I was feeling so proud and happy, I just said something to the effect that I didn't think there could be two directors of post-production.

The Public Premier

Once it was clear that there would be no acceptance to a festival, I thought that there should be at least one public showing. The least expensive place for me to use this time turned out to be the historic Texas Theater in the south of Dallas. It was also the place Johnny and I had gone to do a sound test for the entire movie.

The Texas Theater is where Lee Harvey Oswald fled after assassinating President Kennedy. It is a cavernous place and very old. The acoustics are quite bad and even when it is half full it seems empty.

Due to cost, the showing had to be on a Monday, September 10, 2018 at 5:30 PM, which limited attendance dramatically. That was okay. The people who came were enthusiastic and genuinely pleased with the film. I was a bit sad that my sister did not come, but several of my good friends did. I was particularly happy that one of the extras whom I had invited came and brought his mother. It was nice to think that the film was now partly his too, forever.

One of the happy moments was seeing the film's name on the marquee. This had not been possible for the private showing for cast and crew.

Reactions To The Film

As can be expected, the reactions to the completed film were diverse. Some people were disappointed; others gave it high praise and found it very entertaining.

During one of the final run-throughs of the sound for *Revenge In Kind*, I asked Johnny Marshall what he thought of the movie now that it was finished. He knows so much about film and I respect his talent and knowledge so very much that I placed great value on his opinion. Also, I was absolutely sure that he would tell me the truth.

He paused, seemingly to think about how to be diplomatic. He said the screenplay had a huge promise. He had liked it a lot when he first read it because it was creepy, fast-paced, and the story line is really relevant. But the film came off less so on all three counts, he said.

I wanted to know what he thought the main failings were, so I pushed him. He said that the acting was a mixed bag, with some pretty strong performances, but others that were weak. Also, he felt the action scenes were not particularly well done. I replied that several people had tried to edit the action scenes, to which he said the problem probably could not have been fixed with editing, it was the execution of the action itself.

Johnny's critique was somewhat in the middle, with more opinionated views on either side. On the negative end was a reviewer of a draft of the movie who taught film school in Los Angeles. He called me to say that I should delete the majority of the film, especially all the action, and just turn it into a short film.

There were middle-of-the-road responses, too, of course. My cousin Fred damned it with faint praise saying it "wasn't too bad" and gave it a 6 on a 10-point scale in an online rating. That mildly irked me, in part, because it violated my own sense of loyalty. When I saw it, I recalled a similar situation of my own when another cousin of mine had asked me to rate her daughter's music in an online poll. I didn't even need to listen to it; because she was family, she was a perfect 10. Now you can argue that such is not honest, but in my own panoply of values, there is a time when you can harmlessly dispense with objectivity. Now you could ask, why should I have expected anything different, given his decision to forego the directorship? Fair point. But in that regard, I note something I have always remembered that Thumper said in the film *Bambi*, which I saw when I was very young. He said, "If you can't say something nice, then don't say nothin' at all."

There were also very favorable responses to the film, many by professionals. The published reviews by film critics—all two of them—were pretty positive as well. Before I present them to you, let me say that I did not know either of the reviewers and do not have any connections to anyone who does know them. They were not paid, and I had no editorial control over them whatsoever.

The first review was done by Cinapse.com, an online film review site. The second one appeared in the *Daily Illini*, the student newspaper of the University of Illinois at Champaign-Urbana. The latter undoubtedly appeared because I was an alumna of the school. Although the year of the date in the *Daily Illini* article says 2017, the review actually appeared in 2018.

As for my own feelings about the film, I have two observations. One was best voiced by Zubi, who said a key takeaway about the film is that we actually completed what we started. He said that so very many films—most, in fact—never make it to the finish line. While *Revenge In Kind* may not be among the best movies ever made, it is certainly among the movies made.

My second observation is that I think that this movie, which is a true independent with no association with studios or experienced production companies, turned out to be better than more than half of the movies I watch (or that I start and then quit out of boredom). And, I will add in this regard, viewers do tend to watch the film all the way through, as is clear from the streaming statistics. That people find it worth watching shows that people find it entertaining.

Filming An Indie

Rod Machen
Writer living in Austin, Texas
Feb 2 · 2 min read

REVENGE IN KIND: Murder in Big D
Texas-based film gets gritty in the city.

What happens when the victim becomes the victimizer? This is the question posed by *Revenge in Kind*, a Texas production that explores the darker side of the human equation.

Brooding police officer Chris Coxon (Chad Halbrook) joins together with criminal psychologist Sarah Scott (Sasha Higgins) to solve a series of violent attacks against women. In the meantime, perpetrators of sexual violence are showing up dead. It's a conundrum the two struggle to figure out.

In between case files, the two develop a romantic relationship. This isn't a love story, but once they get past their initial jitters, the chemistry works well. Their connection also allows for a final-act plot twist that serves the story well.

Tom Heard plays the main psychopath of the tale, and he's the type of person it would be best to cross the street to avoid making eye contact. He's creepy, as well as hulking, with a shaven head. His stalking is a little obvious, but he creates menace every time he's on screen.

Shot in Dallas, *Revenge in Kind* exudes the modern-day Lone Star State in all its multi-faceted glory. From tiny bungalows to a shiny office complex, the film will feel authentic to every viewer from the state. There's even some Tex-Mex thrown in for good measure.

For fans of grindhouse and exploitation films, *Revenge in Kind* offers a small indie version of those genres. Filmmaker KC Bailey and director Roger Lindley have woven together a dark tale about the menace of modern life.

Definitely, lock your doors.

MOVIE REVIEW

'Revenge in Kind' casts critical eye on current issues

Bailey's debut film brings to light issues of violence, assault

BY MARK TOLEDANO
STAFF WRITER

They say revenge is a dish best served cold.

For the characters in "Revenge in Kind," this is an understatement. Writer-producer K.C. Bailey, a University alumna, showcases her talent in her debut film, a psychological thriller rich with twists and surprises.

Embattled police detective Chris Coxon (Chad Halbrook) takes on the case of a serial killer who preys on unsuspecting women. As the hunters wind up hunted themselves, Coxon falls head-over-heels for the police department's new criminal profiler, Sarah Scott (Sasha Higgins), a brilliant woman of mysterious origins. But does she have something to hide? Does he? As the two crack the case together, revelations into both of their personal lives open up new angles that lead to a shocking finale.

The opening of the movie sets the mood throughout. Confusion overwhelms the characters as they are introduced. One by one, they are thrust onto the screen with terrified eyes, throbbing hearts and blistering fury. We don't need to know their backstory to understand their pain; their desperation is palpable.

Role reversal is central to

PHOTO COURTESY OF PONO PRODUCTIONS
Chad Halbrook is Detective Chris Coxon on the set of "Revenge in Kind." Director K.C. Bailey's debut film casts a critical eye on current hot topics, including violence against men and women.

the film. Victims become victimizers and perpetrators are perpetrated. Fans of Quentin Tarantino will quickly identify with other revenge films like "Inglourious Basterds"

and "Death Proof." But unlike Tarantino's style, "Revenge in Kind" does not present bloody carnage just for the fun of it. The violence in the film is raw and necessary. Characters clearly display the harm that is inflicted upon them. Women are victims. Men are victims.

"Violence is not gender-based," Bailey said. "It is a

human phenomenon, not just a gender phenomenon."

The timing of the film is just right. The subject matter — dealing heavily with sexual assault against women — coincides with the #MeToo movement. In one scene, a lawyer asks a job applicant to "walk around a little" after he prods her on what she would normally wear to work. Such scenes of workplace harassment bring to mind the sexual misconduct scandals that took down the careers of powerful men like Harvey Weinstein and Roy Moore.

It is refreshing to see a film enter the political conversation without being preachy. There is no doubt that the events in the film were inspired by real social issues. But, like all good political films, "Revenge in Kind" does not give straightforward answers to complicated problems.

Take the scene where a serial rapist breaks into a woman's house. She grabs her gun for protection. What happens next plays out exactly like you think it would. Some people would read this as the empowerment women obtain by arming themselves; others might view it as a commentary on gun violence. All opinions aside, the fact is Bailey has brilliantly woven together two issues dominating the national conversation in a way that forces us to think critically about both.

Skillfully crafted, Bailey's film begs questions. It is the type of movie that encourages its audience to connect the events in the film to society at large, the fictional characters to real people living real lives. The beauty of indie films like "Revenge in Kind" is they are more personal and relatable due to their lack of special effects. The issues raised in the film are important ones that cannot be ignored.

buzz factor: ★ ★ ★ ★

markjt2@readbuzz.com

Chapter 24: Wrapping Up

I have a few more observations to share that have no consistent theme to link them, so this chapter will be a little disjointed. Hopefully it will tie up some loose ends and thus be a good ending to the diary.

Coda For Pono

Shortly after the film was released in December 2017, Pono's health took a turn for the worse. Her glucose readings were increasingly erratic, making it harder to be confident that I was not giving her too much or too little insulin. I tried to keep my spirits up because I was afraid that she could sense my sadness and fear of losing her. She kept close to me even more than in the past. I was grateful that she still felt like moving enough to be with me. Every night I helped her onto our bed, although she had for some time had her own little staircase to assist her getting up.

It was mid-April when I awoke to find her not with me. I went to the hall closet where she sometimes went when she was afraid of lightning and thunder. She lay there in a pool of her own urine. She could not stand up. I took her in my arms and gently cleaned her, then went through our blood testing, insulin, and feeding. Her appetite was now failing.

Throughout the day I could tell she did not feel well. She mostly slept but appeared so piteous when awake. As anyone who confronts the death of a loved one knows, the sorrow is unfathomable. My insides cringed and I felt constantly on the verge of tears. The day would come soon that she would no longer be *there*.

I stroked her often over a couple of days, talking softly and telling her stories of her life and how she had always been the bravest, most independent cat I had known. One of my favorites was when she was about three years old and had accompanied me and my husband out to the orchard where we were picking limes to fill a large order that had come in. As we prepared to return to the garage to box them, we saw a huge German Shepherd come onto the property. He was trotting straight toward Pono. My husband and I simultaneously yelled to try to scare the dog away, fearful that he would grab our 8-pound cat and kill her.

The dog kept coming. Pono stood still, her back arched and fur standing up. I screeched, "Pono run!" Well, that is exactly what she did. But she tore out running straight for the dog. She was closing the gap between them fast when the dog froze, then turned and ran the opposite direction. She chased him to the edge of our property and stopped. I am sure the hearts of all four of us were beating as fast as possible. Pono finally turned and sauntered to us, seemingly quite proud of herself.

A few days after Pono's decline had begun precipitously, I felt that ending her increasing physical agony was more important than forestalling my mental and spiritual agony. It was time to euthanize her.

On the morning I was to take her to the vet, April 24, 2018, I was well aware of the way I would feel that night. As I took care of her that morning, I was melting inside with grief. I touched her warm body, knowing it would no longer hold life in but a few hours. Making myself put her in the carrier, into the car, and then into the vet's office was done on autopilot. I felt numb.

That night I placed her body carefully into a cleared shelf in my refrigerator. The following day I researched for pet cremation services. I wanted one that would be willing to cremate her alone so that I would be sure that the ashes I received would be hers, with only trace residue from others. Only one of the four places I called would do this and allow me to observe that they actually did it.

The crematorium was about an hour away and I was hardly conscious of the drive. Once there, thankfully, I was the only client and Pono's was the only body. The whole process took about an hour and the people were fairly nice, although jaded. They had some boxes for sale for the ashes, but I liked the free one best for its simplicity and the fact that it was cedar, which I thought might last awhile.

I mixed some of my husband's ashes with Pono's as I knew he would wish. Then I started arrangements to take her remains home, back to Hawai'i where she was born and lived most of her 18 years. I wanted to inter her right next to our other cat, Miki, on the property that was once our home.

The successor owner to our property graciously agreed to allow me to bury Pono there and even let me stay in their guest quarters. It was my first time back to Hawai'i since my husband had died in 2012, so it was an emotional journey for that reason as well.

On the morning of her funeral, I rose and collected plumeria petals from around the property and readied them for the ceremony. I stood looking at the ocean from near her favorite napping place and said prayers of thanks to Nature for her life and the gift of my deep love for her.

Once again, I pondered the question that had so often occurred since my husband's death: is the horror and pain of losing those whom you love so deeply equal to the love and joy of having them in life? Is it better to have loved and lost, or never to have loved at all? Of course, I really knew the answer was that I am the luckiest person to have had my loves, yet at the time I was consumed with grief.

The owner of our old property attended Pono's funeral. I said a few things for and to Pono, thanking her for the gifts of joy she gave, and told her how much I would miss her always. It was a beautiful farewell to one of the greatest cats I have ever known.

A Few Questions Answered

I am often asked what the film cost. I am not willing to reveal that, which is strange perhaps in that I am willing to state my age, 71, and various other personal details. But what I will share is that we went over budget by at least 60% and that subsequent to finishing the film, I have continued to invest in making sure the film is available for streaming.

The top sheet done before the film to try to estimate the cost was a good guide. Yet there were too many big-ticket items that we did not anticipate for our low-budget endeavor, including insurance, attorneys' fees, taxes, and unplanned costs associated with locations and equipment. There were also underestimates, particularly with truck and car rentals. The top sheet was most accurate with regard to personnel costs.

My advice to any independent filmmaker is that they carefully look at the excellent budgeting software available for movies, and that they first, absolutely first, look into hiring an accountant—one that has experience with film production.

Another question I get is whether I ever heard from the Texas Film Commission again. I did not and didn't expect to. Nevertheless, it remains an oddity to me that one of the biggest institutional obstacles to our film was the entity paid for by taxpayers to help filmmakers, and that they had no interest in our product.

A third question is, once the film was finished, were there any big surprises? While I cannot say there were any really unusual surprises, I did not expect to have to continue dealing with taxes for as long as I did. I will elaborate on this a bit, only because at the end of my explanation, I have a word of advice for filmmakers.

We had employees on the film from Texas, Nevada, Louisiana, New York, California, and Georgia. We did everything according to law, paying payroll and state taxes as required. After the film was completed, all of the states continued to ping me to try to get more taxes. I sent letters repeatedly explaining that my employment of cast and crew was short-term and one-time-only, therefore I did not owe more taxes.

All states eventually got it except California. I even got phone calls from them threatening me with fines. I ended up filing a form to terminate taxation twice and then still getting a bill. Seriously, I think I spent over 20 hours of my time trying to turn off the spigot of tax collection attempts.

California was unique in another regard. It has developed an incredibly efficient system to go after those who don't pay due alimony and child support. There was one Texas resident whom I hired for one afternoon of acting. Apparently, he once lived in California and had children and a former spouse still living there. Through my paying taxes on him, California learned that he had earned income. They wanted me to garnish his wages. I had to explain that I had only paid him for three hours. They sent me another form to fill out.

A few weeks after settling the above-noted child-support dodger, I got another inquiry from California on the same subject, this one about an actress. I settled this one a bit easier having had the experience of the first dodger. It surprised me a bit that a woman would owe child support, although I guess it shouldn't have.

I would give the following advice to any filmmaker who is going to pay taxes as they should: try to minimize the number of states from which you hire people in order to avoid filing with each one. The paperwork will be drastically reduced if you hire only from one or two states. If you do use people from multiple states, set aside time for dealing with follow-up tax issues.

The fourth question is what my most memorable experience in making the movie was. This one is really hard to answer because I have so many rich memories, some of which I have already shared with you. I think the most honest answer is that the most memorable thing is not a single experience at all. Instead, it is a whole set of experiences that led up to one single phenomena: that I came to like, admire, and respect Angel so much.

Were it not for the joint endeavor to make the film, Angel is not a person I would likely ever have become close to because there was no overlap in our lives. If we had met at a cocktail party, for example, I doubt we would have even conversed much, as there would have been no commonality of experiences, dreams, or even personalities. Thus, it was quite a lesson to me that someone so different from me in so many respects could become someone whom I hold dear, someone whom I would like to remain a part of my life.

Coming to love someone as a friend—and I am not talking about quick passion here, but a deep respect and genuine affection—is very often a product of time. This is because it can take years to accumulate the experiences with another person that enable us to know and understand one another. For this reason, it is often friends we have known longest, and those with whom we share memories, whom we love.

But time is not the only factor that can forge a basis for love. Being plunged into an ordeal with someone and surviving hardships together can anneal a relationship, enabling love as deep as that engendered by time. Going though war together is a well-known example. In the case of me and Angel, we went through an intense, time-compressed, highly creative venture together. We were immersed in the project, living it and breathing it for months.

The flavor of deep friendship can be determined by other emotions as well. In my case with Angel, it is tinged with gratitude. I had a dream to make the movie my way, and the desire to experience every element of its making. Angel understood that and not only helped make the dream come true, he made sure that my experiences of the process were fulsome and, to the extent he could, joyful.

I am not claiming that everything was rosy between us. He did disappoint me at times, as I am sure I did him. But overall, making the movie was an experience like no other—exhilarating, frustrating, wild, and deeply eye-opening. And Angel helped make it happen like no one else could have or would have. I got to know a lot about him in the process, including that he is a man of integrity and honor. All of this is why I will be his friend forever.

What Next

Although I have written a few non-fiction books, I also wrote a novel entitled *Death For Cause*. This book pre-dated my writing *Revenge In Kind*, which was, in first form, a screenplay and not a novel at all. Between the two works of fiction, I have always thought that *Death For Cause* was the better story.

When at last *Revenge In Kind* was up on a big screen, I knew the adventure was mostly over. It was my hope, however, that the film would either make money (which it has not), or that the script would be discovered by a studio and a high-level production of it would be make (which has not happened either).

Staying with the dream for a minute, let me tell you what was supposed to happen next in this made-up scenario. The kudos that *Revenge In Kind* would garner would lead to bigger things, namely big-studio interest in *Death For Cause*. Then, according to this dream, I would be asked to assist in turning the novel into a screenplay.

Filming An Indie

Working on *Death For Cause* (in a pre-pandemic environment anyway) was to be super exciting because it takes place in locations around the globe, from steamy slums in Manila to high-brow clubs in Manhattan.

I am pretty sure that my dreams for further films will be just that—dreams. If there has been one thread of truth throughout my life it is that dreams-come-true do not occur to me because of luck or happenstance. I have almost always made my own magic, sometimes with help, but often alone (or just with my muse). In other words, making reality of fancy is hard work for me.

In closing, I will share a comparison I thought of after the film was done. I recalled how I felt with the death of Pono, when I wondered if the agony of losing her was worth the joy of love while she lived, and whether it would have been better to simply not to have had the experience at all. If you never love, then you don't really know what you missed. If you don't love, then you do not suffer the everlasting grief and longing engendered by death.

Making the film was also an emotional ordeal, although of a much different quality and scale. It left me with some painful memories of anger, isolation, mistakes, and ego bruises. And certainly, if I had not done it, I would be richer now in terms of money. But, like having the joy of loving someone, making art gives life meaning and depth. And, as Ed told me when he agreed to let us shoot at his house, doing unusual things give you something to talk about. Making Revenge In Kind gave me a rich experience that was totally unusual and is certainly something to talk about.

Appendix: List Of My Activities

If you contemplate making a film, the following list may be useful in understanding the duties that you may need to undertake. Some items are specific to *Revenge In Kind*, but similar activities may be required for other filmmaking. This list is of my own activities; it does not include the myriad things that Angel, Zubi, and others accomplished, which would make a book in itself.

Set Up

- Formed legal entity for film (researched LLCs; filed all legal papers with City, County, and State; paid all fees).
- Filed copyright transfer with US Government for script for Pono Productions.
- Registered script with western screenwriters association.
- Set up bank account, credit card; obtained debit cards for film departments.
- Set up Google Drive, email accounts for key personnel, and for casting purposes.
- Met with city officials, attorneys, company or site representatives numerous times to secure permissions.
- Researched & designed Nondisclosure Agreement for script.
- Set up FedEx account.

Insurance

- Interviewed multiple insurance companies; researched & selected insurance parameters.
- Obtained and delivered all Insurance Certificates for locations.
- Obtained Errors & Omissions Insurance (separate from above).

- Researched & interviewed companies and contracted with one for Script Clearance.
- Worked with equipment companies to remove supplemental insurance.

Locations

- Scouted for locations, visiting hundreds online and dozens in reality.
- Selected sites used for filming & coordinated film schedules with owners.
- Researched/drafted location agreement template; wrote Use Agreement for all sites; obtained signatures and made payments.

Artwork

- Interviewed sculptors, potters, iron-work artists for Coxon's artwork.
- Worked with chosen artist to research and design Nyx bust.
- Scheduled and set up photography exhibit for gallery scene.

Casting and Crew Selection

- Selected film Producer.
- Interviewed candidates for director, cinematographer, production designer; and made final decisions on all.
- Set up system and folders for all incoming emailed cast & crew applications.
- Read every incoming email (hundreds) and filed each by job(s) sought.
- Reviewed all online casting applications and, with director, selected ones for audition.
- Wrote follow-up inquiry emails to all applicants of interest.
- Arranged auditions location and set-up.
- Recruited/managed assistants and readers for auditions.
- Arranged food for auditions sessions.
- Prepared rating sheet for evaluating auditions and kept records of responses.
- Participated as 1 of 3 in evaluating each audition and key applicants for crew.
- Set up and kept all files for paper records for auditions.
- Interfaced with talent agencies; key contact for Horne Agency.

Contracts

- Prepared all contracts for cast and crew.

- Prepared all contracts and records for vendors.
- Interfaced with City of Mesquite and Mesquite Police Dept. on all film issues.
- Prepared proposal for Dallas Regional Medical Center; obtained contract.

Production

- Worked with production designer on ideas for set design.
- Worked with director on dialog and script re-work.
- Worked with director and stunt choreographer to develop ending scene.
- Provided key input to correct makeup, hair, and wardrobe problems.
- Input on-scene.

Accounting & Payroll

- Helped identify and interview accountant.
- Set up Quickbooks account and entered most cast, crew, and vendor information.
- Worked with accountant on all payments and Quickbooks transfer.
- Kept track of invoices, wrote vendor checks, kept records.
- Wrote and delivered all payroll.
- Set up filing system for all employees and 1099's and kept files.
- Paid taxes employment taxes in TX, NY, NV, LA, and CA.
- Took over input and reconciling Quickbooks starting with post-production.
- Reconciled cast, crew, vendor files with accountant.
- Budget tracking and reconciliation starting with week 3 of production.
- Filed w-2s and 1099s.
- Paid state and federal taxes.

Film Editing

- Interviewed potential editors as 1 of 3 interviewers.
- Selected Editor and negotiated rate and contract.
- Supervised editing of assembly and all iterations of film cuts (>600 hours of editing work).
- Recruited panel members and set up panels for film cut reviews.
- Input credit roll information and checked names against contracts.

Filming An Indie

Sound Designer/Mixer and Composer

- Interviewed potential sound designer/mixers.
- Selected Sound designer/mixer and negotiated rate and contract.
- Identified and interviewed several composers.
- Selected library of sample sounds to use as guides.
- Selected Composer and negotiated rate and contract.
- Researched and selected all source music artists; wrote and obtained Licenses.

Distribution

- Researched and interviewed film aggregators.
- Selected and contracted with Distribber.
- Researched and selected outlet platforms.
- Worked with Distribber on specifications and submission.
- Selected regions for distribution.
- Ended contract with Distribber.
- Researched and interviewed 4 other aggregators.
- Selected Walla (Mojo) and replicated above with them.
- Managed takedown of contract with Walla and recontract with Bitmax.

Trailer, Poster, and Titles

- Researched trailer houses and interviewed 12.
- Negotiated price and contract with Wheelhouse Creative.
- Provided all image inputs for poster; worked with designer to create.
- Provided creative input and selected output on trailer and titles.
- Resized poster in Photoshop for 3 streaming platforms per specs.

DVD/Blu-Ray Production

- Interviewed several firms for DVD/Blu-Rays; selected Allied Vaughn.
- Researched theft prevention technologies and pricing.
- Provided input, QC, and oversight of jewel case design.

Subtitles

- Researched and selected subtitle/cc company, BTI Studios [later Iyuno Media Group].
- Acted as intermediary on numerous QC issues between BTI and Allied Vaughn.
- Reviewed CC for entire film for quality control.
- Worked with Bitmax and Iyuno on foreign language .stl files.

Public Relations

- Kept Facebook account and Pono Production website.
- Prepared still photos in Photoshop.
- Issued press releases on production.
- Drafted articles for press and handled interviews.

Acknowledgements

I am thankful to Anna Fisher Kruse who edited the draft with care and great skill. I also thank Steve Kite and Laurie Kidder for reading and commenting on a draft of the diary. As always, responsibility for errors is the author's alone.

Made in the USA
Middletown, DE
02 April 2023

28054173R00129